Music in Worship

MUSIC IN WORSHIP

W. MORRIS FORD

Convention Press

NASHVILLE   TENNESSEE

© 1960 • CONVENTION PRESS

NASHVILLE, TENNESSEE

511-01917

Church Study Course for Teaching and Training.
This book is number 1917 in category 19, section A.
Library of Congress Catalog Card Number: 60-8736
Printed in the United States of America
5. AT 60 R.R.D.

Contents

About the Author

W. MORRIS FORD is a native of Illinois, born March 16, 1908. Receiving his high school education in Patterson, Illinois, he completed the A. B. degree at Southwestern at Memphis, Tennessee. Dr. Ford attended the Southern Baptist Theological Seminary in Louisville, Kentucky, where he earned the Th. M. and Ph. D. degrees. He also holds honorary doctorates from Baylor University and East Texas Baptist College.

Dr. Ford has been pastor of four churches, serving the Speed Memorial Church, Speed, Indiana, during his seminary days; the Calvary Baptist Church, Kansas City, Missouri; the First Baptist Church, Jackson, Tennessee; and his present church, the First Baptist Church, Longview, Texas.

Many distinguished positions of denominational leadership have been held by Dr. Ford. He served as a member of the Board of Trustees of Southern Baptist Seminary, Southwest Baptist College, Union University, Baylor University, and East Texas Baptist College of which he is currently serving his fourth year as president. In addition, he has served on Baptist state boards in Missouri, Tennessee, and Texas, as well as numerous committees.

Dr. Ford comes from a musical family dating back nearly one hundred years. He is the possessor of a rich, well-trained bass voice which he has used in civic operas, concerts, and oratorios in addition to his church music. This book *Music in Worship* has come out of a background of personal study and experience. Dr. Ford has recorded one long-play album by Word Records titled *Songs of Assurance*.

Dr. and Mrs. Ford have one son, David, who is also a musician studying for his Master of Music degree at Baylor University.

Church Study Course for Teaching and Training

THE CHURCH STUDY COURSE for Teaching and Training began October 1, 1959. It is a merger of three courses previously promoted by the Baptist Sunday School Board—the Sunday School Training Course, the Graded Training Union Study Course, and the Church Music Training Course.

The course is fully graded. The system of awards provides a series of five diplomas of twenty books each for Adults or Young People, one diploma of ten books for Young People, two diplomas of five books each for Intermediates, and two diplomas of five books each for Juniors. All book awards earned previously in the Sunday School Training Course, the Graded Training Union Study Course, and the Church Music Training Course may be transferred to the new course.

The purpose of the course is to help Christians grow in knowledge and conviction, to help them grow toward maturity in Christian character and competence for service, to encourage them to participate worthily as workers in their churches, and to develop leaders for all phases of church life and work.

The Church Study Course for Teaching and Training is promoted by the Baptist Sunday School Board, 127 Ninth Avenue, North, Nashville, Tennessee, through its Sunday School, Training Union, Church Music, and Church Administration departments and by the Sunday School, Training Union, and Church Music departments of the states affiliated with the Southern Baptist Convention. A complete description of the course and the system of awards may be found in the *Church Study Course for Teaching and Training* catalog which may be obtained without charge from any one of these departments.

A record of all awards earned should be maintained in each church. A person should be designated by the church to keep the files. Forms for such records may be ordered from any Baptist Book Store.

Requirements for Credit in Class
or Home Study

If CREDIT is desired for the study of this book in a class or by home study the following requirements must be met:

I. In Classwork

1. The class must meet a minimum of seven and one-half clock hours. The required time does not include assembly periods. Ten class periods of forty-five minutes each are recommended. (If laboratory or clinical work is desired in specialized or technical courses, this requirement may be met by six clock hours of classwork and three clock hours of supervised laboratory or clinical work.)

2. A class member who attends all class sessions and completes the reading of the book within a week following the last class session will not be required to do any written work.

3. A class member who is absent from one or more class sessions must answer the questions on all chapters he misses. In such a case, he must turn in his paper within a week, and he must certify that he has read the book.

4. The teacher should request an award for himself. A person who teaches a book in section B, C, or D of any category or conducts an approved unit of instruction for Nursery, Beginner, or Primary children will be granted an award in category 11, Special Studies, which will count as an elective on his own diploma. He should specify in his request the name of the book taught, or the unit conducted for Nursery, Beginner, or Primary children.

5. The teacher should complete the "Request for Book Awards —Class Study" (Form 150) and forward it within two weeks after the completion of the class to the Church Study Course Awards Office, 127 Ninth Avenue, North, Nashville 3, Tennessee.

II. In Home Study

1. A person who does not attend any class session may receive credit by answering all questions for written work as indicated in

the book. When a person turns in his paper on home study, he must certify that he has read the book.

2. Students may find profit in studying the text together, but individual papers are required. Carbon copies or duplicates in any form cannot be accepted.

3. Home study work papers may be graded by the pastor or a person designated by him, or they may be sent to the Church Study Course Awards Office for grading. The form entitled "Request for Book Awards—Home Study" (Form 151) must be used in requesting awards. It should be mailed to Church Study Course Awards Office 127 Ninth Avenue, Nashville 3, Tennessee.

III. Credit for This Book

This book is number 1917 in category 19, section A.

W. HINES SIMS

Secretary, Church Music Department
Baptist Sunday School Board

How to Use This Book

RECENT YEARS have witnessed a revival of interest in music and its close association with services of worship. In the past, many people thought of music merely as a prelude to worship—the periphery of individual and collective participation. With a program of training, plus worship services that call for more active participation of the masses of people through the medium of music, the scene has changed.

Today, music is considered an active, vital part of worship. We actually worship while participating in music. No longer is it regarded as an appendage, a subsidiary, an extra, or an exercise that is indirectly related to a worship experience. We have progressed to the point where there is a realization that we often receive the greatest blessing in our worship as we sing the hymns and hear the beautiful music. The reading of the Scriptures and the messages from God's Word become more vital and meaningful as a result of the effective use of music. Music that is wisely selected, properly interpreted, and appropriately related to each step of the worship service can give it unity as nothing else can.

Much value can come from regular meetings held by those responsible for worship services. At such meetings the leaders make long-range plans for future services and finalize details for services scheduled for the immediate period. They have opportunity to relate each feature of the service to the whole and to relate all services to seasonal, denominational, and local emphases. The music leaders may then select appropriate music and make adequate preparation.

This book has been prepared to give guidance in the proper use of music in services of worship. It defines the functions of those charged with the responsibility for planning services from week to week and then proceeds with practical suggestions for fulfilling them. There are various ways that a book of this type can be used. The following plans are suggested.

1. This is not a technical book on music, and therefore, laymen, as well as musicians, will find it profitable reading. Worship services everywhere would take on added inspiration and meaning if each church member would read this text. Therefore, it is suggested that it be emphasized for home study.

2. This is a book that will appeal to those desiring to form special study groups. Such class sessions can be arranged for the convenience of the majority and can be extended over the necessary period of time to meet credit requirements.

3. A class including those persons having specific responsibilities related to various phases of planning and implementing worship services will benefit greatly from a joint study of this text. This class may include ushers, custodians, and others indirectly concerned, since their responsibilities are a contributing factor to effective worship services.

4. Where the church staff is of sufficient size, a collective study of the book would be profitable. Such a study should include the pastor, minister of music, and minister of education, as well as others having specific responsibilities related to worship services; other staff members who may have indirect responsibilities or assist in various ways. Under the leadership of the pastor, or some other qualified teacher, such a class can be most beneficial.

5. Since the choir, the director, and the organist are such integral parts of each worship service, there would be many values in forming a class that would include these persons, as well as others having similar duties who should be enlisted to attend.

6. Because worship services affect so many people, and because the entire church shares in the responsibility for making the services meaningful and spiritually uplifting, this book should be taught as frequently as possible in all regularly scheduled study courses until all members have been helped.

7. Since the pastor is usually the leader of worship, it is suggested that he teach this book periodically to his church or to one of the special study groups. At other times, the minister of music, minister of education, or some other qualified person may serve as teacher.

A careful study of this book will enable each person to more fully understand the fine art of worship through music. It should serve only as a steppingstone for further and more detailed study on the part of both leaders and laymen as we see the unfolding potential of music as a medium of worship.

LOREN R. WILLIAMS

Editor, Church Music Materials
Church Music Department
Baptist Sunday School Board

CHAPTER 1 OUTLINE

    I. THE MEANING OF WORSHIP

   II. WORSHIP IN THE OLD TESTAMENT

  III. WORSHIP IN THE NEW TESTAMENT

  IV. LATER DEVELOPMENT

   V. LEADERSHIP IN WORSHIP

1

Public Worship

WORSHIP is primarily an inner experience. Because of this, private, personal worship is natural and normal. Despite man's fall, there is within him a spiritual hunger and thirst which draws him to God. If it is true that "man is incurably religious," it is because he was made "in the likeness and image of God." The purpose of this study is to explore some of the many facets of public worship and to emphasize the use of music in worship.

I. THE MEANING OF WORSHIP

There are various types of worship. Some of it is so primitive and coarse that it is repulsive to those of higher sensibilities and training. One person will find his stimulation in the harsh sounds and discords of crude instruments and voices, various incantations and bodily movements. Another will respond only to the pipe organ or the symphony of sound from a choir of trained voices.

1. What Is Worship?

Worship is the response of man to the revelation of God himself. This, worded just a little differently, can be said even of the worship practices of non-Christians. That is to say, worship is the response of man to God as he understands him. Since our purpose is to study Christian worship, we shall use neither time nor space to examine heathen worship with its superstition and frenzy.

It was a worship experience that changed the course of

1

Isaiah's life. There is no better example of true worship. God took the initiative. Isaiah responded, evidently, just as God desired.

First there was the feeling of awe and wonder in the holy Presence which caused the young worshiper to respond spiritually to the heavenly voices singing "Holy, holy, holy."

Then followed the confession of sin. It was a confession which recognized personal and social sins: "Woe is me! for I am undone; because I am a man of unclean lips, and I dwell in the midst of a people of unclean lips: for mine eyes have seen the King, the Lord of hosts" (Isa. 6:5).

The third part was the experience of God's cleansing and redeeming grace. The worshiper, by faith, accepted that which the Lord graciously bestowed.

Finally, Isaiah dedicated his life to God's service with a courageous and magnanimous, "Here am I; send me."

This is worship! Private worship in a public service; the response of one worshiper in the midst of the congregation. So shall it ever be. The one who attends public worship is led to think of God, the Holy One, the Father, mighty to save. He is then led to think of himself, the needy one, seeing himself as God sees him. Having found the answer to his personal need, his mind turns to others who need the redeeming grace. He prays, gives, sends, or even goes—in a spirit like that of Isaiah.

2. *Attitudes in Worship*

The word "attitude" has two meanings. The first is "position of the body, as suggesting some thought, feeling, or action." The second is "state of mind, behaviour, or conduct regarding some matter, as indicating opinion or purpose." The two are very closely related, as is readily seen. The behaviour and even the bodily position of the worshiper are the result of the thought and feeling.

There is no definite Bible teaching concerning physical attitudes in worship. Even Jesus did not follow a careful pattern of conduct in prayer and worship. The emotional response in each case dictated the physical response. He stood to pray, but not always. He prostrated himself, but not always. In the house of worship he evidently yielded to custom, standing to read the Scriptures, sitting to speak to the congregation.

The fact that one kneels to pray does not necessarily mean that he is more in earnest than the one who does not kneel. Great need often drives one to his knees, but kneeling does not always drive one to prayer. We need to be very careful about forcing outward forms upon folk who are not "kneeling in the heart."

Worship, then, does not mean outward acts. It does mean an inner response to God which may result in outward manifestations.

3. *Forms of Worship*

Although "man is incurably religious," the damage suffered in the Fall (Genesis 3) forever impaired his spiritual grasp. Man has always worshiped, yet does not worship easily. He approaches God with timidity and even with great difficulty. Needy man! Always he needs help. Perhaps he needs help to worship more than he needs any other one thing.

Worship in the first century was definitely spiritual, and the artistic element was subordinate. By A.D. 476 a complete reversal had come about under the strong influence of the Roman Catholic Church. The temptation was to forget that worship was religious. The Mass was religious drama in its most artistic form. The leaders dropped far behind the simplicity of the early churches to the Old Testament pageantry and drama. There were vestments, bells, ablutions, processions, prayers for the dead, and frequent changes in posture

—all in the interest of worship. Latin continued to be used, even among other peoples, until it was accepted by some as a divine tongue.

The Reformation brought a change. Soon worshipers were divided into three camps—those at the two extremes and the ones on middle ground. The Lutherans and Episcopalians kept all that they considered worthy in the system of worship. They use a modified liturgical service.

The opposite extreme found the Quakers, some Baptists, and a few Methodists caring nothing for artistic forms. In the center are Presbyterians, Congregationalists, Reformed Churches, most Baptists, and most Methodists.

It is our conviction that we are safer in the middle of the road in this matter. Extreme formality kills the spirit. Extreme informality dishonors God. The wise use of the means of worship and the aids to worship will keep Christ in the center, the Bible in the center, preaching and music in that same center!

II. Worship in the Old Testament

There is no doubt that worship is as old as man. In the Garden of Eden we have a picture of unbroken fellowship between God and his creatures before the Fall. Nothing is said about altars or sacrifices until after that tragic experience. The worship on the part of Cain and Abel was something they had learned from their parents. During all those early years of human history, worship of God seems to have been personal and private, though not necessarily secret.

1. *Individual Worship*

The Genesis account reveals the use of an altar and the exercise of individual worship when Noah led his family and all the animals from the ark: "And Noah builded an altar unto the Lord; and took of every clean beast, and of every clean fowl, and offered burnt offerings on the altar" (Gen. 8:20).

Abraham, too, built an altar when he arrived in the land of the Canaanites (Gen. 12:7). Later, when he felt led to sacrifice his son Isaac, he took him to Moriah where an altar had evidently been established for regular sacrificial offerings. "And Abraham said unto his young men, Abide ye here with the ass; and I and the lad will go yonder and worship, and come again to you" (Gen. 22:5).

Worship in its simplest form is revealed in the experience of Eliezer when he went to seek a wife for Isaac. When his heart rejoiced over the discovery of Rebekah who was the exact answer to his seeking, he "bowed down his head, and worshipped the Lord" (Gen. 24:26).

2. Public Worship

But there was also public worship. We hear the psalmist say, "I had gone with the multitude, I went with them to the house of God, with the voice of joy and praise, with a multitude that kept holyday" (Psalm 42:4). At the time of King David's death, he "said to all the congregation, Now bless the Lord your God. And all the congregation blessed the Lord God of their fathers, and bowed down their heads, and worshipped the Lord, and the king" (1 Chron. 29:20).

The development of public worship was most rapid during the days of David and Solomon. The Temple services consisted of four parts: (1) sacrificial acts at regular morning and evening sacrifice and on extraordinary occasions when blood flowed lavishly; (2) ceremonial acts and postures of adoration or reverence when the high priest returned from presenting incense offerings in the holy place, the worshipers prostrating themselves at the sound of the silver trumpets; (3) the service of praise with instruments, vocal song, or both; and (4) public prayer in what was described as shorter forms, half praise, half prayer. An expanded discussion of Temple worship will be given in chapter 2.

III. WORSHIP IN THE NEW TESTAMENT

In the New Testament we find three kinds of public worship. These will be discussed briefly. They are Temple worship, synagogue worship, and Christian worship.

1. *Temple Worship*

The Temple figures prominently in New Testament history. It was there that Zacharias had the vision which assured him that he would not die childless, that his wife Elizabeth would bear a son. It was there also that the aged Simeon and Anna greeted the infant Jesus and sang their great hymns of joy. When he was twelve years of age, he made his first conscious visit to the Temple, where he amazed the Temple rabbis with his understanding, his questions and answers.

Jesus spent much time in the Temple area. There he walked in the Temple courts, taught and disputed with the Jews, observed in the treasury, and cleansed the Court of the Gentiles from the dealers that profaned it. Not being of the priestly class, he never entered the sanctuary, but used the several courts open to laymen.

The actual worship service in New Testament times was almost identical with that described earlier: sacrificial acts, ceremonial acts symbolizing the seeking and receiving of divine favor; praise by the official ministrants of the Temple (sometimes including the people), using trumpets, cymbals, and vocal song; and public prayer in its various forms.

Christian worship did not include the Temple service, but was developed along synagogue lines. The reason is obvious: the whole sacrificial and ceremonial system terminated for Christians with the life and death of Jesus.

2. Synagogue Worship

Because the Temple was so distant from most of the people, it was natural that a local place of worship and instruction would be developed. Each community had its own synagogue ("gathering" or "gathering place"). Some believe it was instituted by Moses, but it is more likely that it came into prominence during the exile. At first the idea was only to use it for the exposition of the law, but later, both prayers and preaching were added. The main emphasis, however, remained upon instruction. The usual service consisted of vocal recitation of Scripture passages and blessings; prayers that were memorized, called the "Eighteen Eulogies," with the congregational "Amen"; the reading of the Law and the Prophets; the sermon, at first purely exposition, but later more devotional in character; and the benediction, always pronounced by a priest with the congregational Amen.

3. Christian Worship

Synagogue worship was probably not abandoned after Pentecost, but private meetings like those held in the upper room flourished. It was not only natural to keep the synagogue pattern, but necessary. The young church could hardly have grown in favor with the people if the leaders had completely withdrawn from the popular worship either in the Temple or the synagogue. The usual gathering place of the Jews also afforded an excellent opportunity for witnessing.

Compare our worship services today with the synagogue order of service, and you will see how Christian people have followed the familiar pattern. The development of music in the service has remained the most outstanding deviation, or perhaps we should say growth. The Jewish Sabbath and the Lord's Day of the Christian became incompatible and resulted in the complete divorcement of the synagogue and the Christian church.

Christians first worshiped in private houses. As a result, the earliest form of church architecture was patterned after private houses.

At first there were two meetings, a public and a private one. The public worship was open, informal, and intensely missionary. At such meetings the unconverted and the inquirers made up a large segment of the congregation. There were frequent conversions in the meetings. It was more like a service during our modern revival meetings. Usually this was a morning service.

The private service, usually in the evening, found the devout Christians together at a meal of their own, called a "love feast," and symbolizing their union and fellowship. Both hymns and prayers were parts of the simple service. The "Lord's Supper" followed according to apostolic instructions (1 Cor. 11:23-28).

The evident order of service for public worship consisted of eight parts: prayer, praise, Scripture reading, instructions, prophesying, speaking in tongues, the benediction, and the kiss of grace. There is need for some elaboration on this order of service.[1]

Praise consisted of the singing of hymns which had been written, usually, by fellow Christians in the congregation. Some psalms were used, but mostly the hymns were testimonies in metrical form.

The reading of Old Testament passages followed. Later, the New Testament writings entered in, especially the letters of Paul.

Instruction was expository preaching. The Scriptures were

---

1. For a full account of public Christian worship read Philip Wendell Crannell's article in the *International Standard Bible Encyclopaedia*, Volume V, pages 3111 and 3112.

expounded from the Christian's viewpoint, even as in the synagogue the leaders had explained the Law.

That which followed is not easy to understand. The prophesying was by anyone who believed that the Holy Spirit had given him a message. It was preaching! To say that there is nothing like it today is to display ignorance of many approaches to the Christian ministry. That kind of "prophesying" and even the "speaking in tongues" are not without their exponents today. Paul had trouble with some of the brethren as we know. Extremes are dangerous in any direction.

After the benediction came the brotherly "kiss of peace" according to Paul's instruction (Rom. 16:16; 1 Cor. 16:20; 2 Cor. 13:12; 1 Thess. 5:26).

The public worship of God in the presence of his people is a vital necessity of the Christian life. The New Testament pattern is completely devoid of the ceremonial and the outward emphasis. We are people of the Bible. Let us follow its pattern.

IV. LATER DEVELOPMENT

The tendency toward ceremonialism was natural. On the one hand, there was the Jewish background of Temple worship with its feasts and sacrifices. On the other hand, there was the highly ritualistic background of the religions of Asia Minor, Greece, Italy, and North Africa. It was next to impossible to keep the Christian service simple and personal as well as Christ-centered.

1. *Ceremonialism and Ritualism*

Just as long as Christianity was persecuted and poverty-stricken, the early Christians were able to hold the line against the advances of formalism. Rome, the tyrant, stood with her foot on the neck of the world. As persecutor, she was Christianity's worst enemy. When she embraced the new religion, she only used the kiss of death. Rome was the conqueror, the tyrant, the architect, the road builder, the playboy of the ancient world. Her gods were many: Zeus, Minerva, Dionysos, Apollo, Diana, Isis, Osiris, Mithra. All had come in from captive lands to add to the many bearing Latin names. Tolerant Rome! She had room for all gods but the true one. Christianity was her mortal enemy. The true God was not acceptable because of his high demands.

With Constantine came many changes. He has been called the first Christian emperor. Was he a Christian? We cannot know. His reforms were good. His acceptance of Christianity at least gave it a thrust outward. But the thrust was also downward! Rome fell, but the damage had been done. The darkness that fell upon the world had just one flickering light, the light of the unadorned gospel. Surrounded by ceremonialism and ritualism, the light was still shining.

2. *Complete Freedom*

We are dealing with extremes. And one is as dangerous as the other. Both are barriers against true worship. The one, gaudy ritualism, is a religion without a heart; perhaps also without a cross in the New Testament sense. The other, a dull, orderless, convictionless, powerless religion without a backbone.

By complete freedom we mean worship without leadership, wherein the devotees express themselves freely and without restraint, having no concern for others. One person, uninvited, takes the floor and harangues the crowd. The apostle Paul, after giving the Corinthian Christians a good lesson concerning worship services, closed his remarks with the admonition, "Let all things be done decently and in order" (1 Cor. 14:40).

The author once attended a morning service in a church in a town of three or four thousand people. The pastor came out thumbing his hymnal, looking for an appropriate song.

He led that song and two others, selecting them at random. There was no church bulletin and evidently no order of service for minister or pianist. There was a prayer and another song, the offering, and a rambling sermon. The choir did not sing, except with the congregation. There was no order, no beauty, and little meaning. That church membership numbered nearly a thousand. A handful of people attended! Is this better than the extreme ritualism?

During the Dark Ages, Old Testament rites became ritual with a sad mixture of heathenism, and New Testament freedom became license. Dark indeed were those years.

3. *A Happy Medium*

We believe we have established a happy medium between the rigid formalism of Romanism and the loose individualism. It can be heard in our music. It can be experienced in our preaching. Here is the proper blending of true religion and true art. Here is worship that is objective, that exalts God and thrusts man out to serve.

V. LEADERSHIP IN WORSHIP

The leader in worship has a priestly function. He is also a prophet. Many of us call him a minister. He is all of these and more. But, truly, there is very little worship without leadership. Now it takes a great deal of "brass," one will say, to claim a ministry for oneself that makes him priest, prophet, and leader. But God is the one who has called man to this high place. It is a humbling and challenging experience. More than that, it is, or should be, so awe-inspiring that it will drive one to his knees and thrust him into the field of service with a fully dedicated life and talent.

1. *Priest*

We are afraid of the term! It has so long kept company with heathen religions. To our ears it smacks of sacerdotalism and magic. But it should not. A priest is a mediator, not in the sense that he does for us what we cannot do for ourselves. But he helps us to bring about a contact with God which will make it possible for us, once that contact is established, to do, by God's grace, what it is God's will and purpose that we should do.

Baptists believe in the "priesthood of the believer"; that is, that each individual has access to God without the mediation of a priest. But Baptists also know that few people worship God in a public worship service without the ministry of a God-called man who somehow reaches one hand to God and one to the people and brings them together in divine fellowship.

When we worship in spirit, not just in word, we lift our hearts to God in adoration and praise, and we receive from him the motive to repentance and consecration. The priestly office of the minister consists in the fact that his stated contact with his people in the services of the church gives him the unique opportunity to make more real to their consciousness the fact of God.

This "priest," as we shall see, knows how to use the Bible, prayer, and music to lead his congregation into a satisfying worship experience.

2. Prophet

A prophet is one who speaks for God. If God gives him a vision of things to come, that is good. Our Heavenly Father has always needed seers. But primarily, the prophet proclaims God's Word. He speaks for God.

To Baptist people, a worship service without a sermon leaves an aching void. It should also be true that a preaching service without worship leaves with the congregation a sense of incompleteness. The minister in his role as priest is the leader in worship; in his prophetic role he is the preacher of God's message.

This man whom God has called must be pastor, teacher, administrator, and statesman, as well as priest and prophet. Rarely is one person capable in all of these fields; but woe unto that minister who fails to be mediator and messenger!

3. Co-ordinator

Finally, the one who leads in public worship must be a co-ordinator. Our main interest in this volume is the part music plays in worship. Much space will be given later to the pastor's part in music and musicians in the total service of worship. The pastor is the one who usually has the basic responsibility of co-ordinating the program parts into an intelligible, inspiring, soul-satisfying whole. Since music is so widely and vitally used in worship services, the minister of music often shares in the responsibility of co-ordinating various parts of the service. Because music is an art requiring specialization and training, it is particularly important that there be a spirit of "rapport" between the pastor and the musicians.

FOR FURTHER STUDY AND DISCUSSION

1. Altars were used in early Old Testament history. Use a good concordance to look up every reference to an altar used in Jehovah worship, and then make a written list of them, giving brief details of the Bible account.
2. Study the Old Testament account of the building of the Temple and of its use in worship. Then turn to the New Testament and look up references to the Temple during Jesus' life.
3. Make a study of the synagogue and the type of worship carried on in the synagogue.
4. Make a study of both priest and prophet until you can make a clear distinction between them as to their life and their work.

CHAPTER 2 OUTLINE

I. THE ANTIQUITY OF MUSIC

II. MUSIC IN OLD TESTAMENT WORSHIP

III. MUSIC IN NEW TESTAMENT WORSHIP

IV. EARLY CHRISTIAN PRACTICES

V. THE DARK YEARS

2

The Origin and Development of Church Music

It is vitally necessary to give a brief history of music in general in order to explain the part music has played and is playing in worship. There is a vast amount of material available. In fact, the great difficulty in such a brief work as this is that of reducing the mass of information to a small, understandable section in this chapter. We shall examine first the non-biblical and then the biblical record.

I. The Antiquity of Music

The use of music in worship is perhaps almost as old as man himself. Let us consider some of the uses and developments of both vocal and instrumental music as revealed in early records.

1. *Non-biblical Record*

Music history begins with instruments. They are classed usually in three forms, but let us depart from the usual and include a fourth, the voice. Is not the voice an instrument? God-given, physical, varying, the voice is a glorious instrument. Actually, it comes third in our outline of four instrumental forms. Let us examine them.

(1) *Percussion instruments.*—The drum type is possibly the oldest under this heading which includes rattles, gongs, triangles, tamtams, castanets, tambourines, and cymbals. All of these are instruments of percussion. Among some peoples

15

the drum was the only instrument. Good examples are the Australian aboriginal tribes and the Eskimos.

No doubt the drum and other percussion instruments came into being in response to man's desire for rhythm. Joy was expressed by the stamping of feet and the clapping of hands. This expanded quickly into the beating of hollow logs, clicking of sticks, and so forth. The drum development was most outstanding in South America. Its influence is still felt.

Drum worship was practiced, and in many parts of the world the percussion instruments played a leading role in pagan worship.

(2) *Wind instruments.*—The development of the pipe type of instrument, which had to be blown, revealed a much higher degree of intellectuality. It is possible that this was a crude type of the horn or trumpet. It joined the drum as a special instrument in warfare to give victory over the enemies. It is known that such an instrument was designed to frighten the foe as well as inspire the warriors. Among some it was believed that it could be used to drive away demons. It even came to be used for "rain making."

Another early pipe instrument was the flute. Just as the trumpet was born for a specific purpose—war—the flute came in response to love. It was the instrument of romance among the Greeks. Even among Indian tribes in North America it was called "the courting-flute."

It is of special interest to learn that the nose instead of the mouth was first used in playing the flute and pipe. We are told that long practice is necessary to learn the art of playing the flute with the mouth, but it can be played easily at the first attempt with the nostril, since the breath comes out at the precise angle necessary to produce the tone.

(3) *The voice.*—When did man start singing? We do not know exactly. It is believed that vocal music originated in impassioned speech. We know that song is an outpouring of

the heart expressing joy, grief, love, hope, despair, and forti-
tude. Impassioned speech is not singing. The range in speech
is severely limited, while the whole range of the voice is used
in singing.

Primitive man was evidently content with one note. This
note in proper rhythm became a chant. Later, another note
was added, then a third, and melody was born. All that man
needed was a start. Soon he was using a five-note scale.
Later the three and the five were joined to make the full octave and to join other octaves. For many, many years, there
was only unison singing with no harmony and, of course, no
written notes.

(4) *Stringed instruments.*—The final classification was the
lyre type of instrument. It was the gift of the Aryan race.
Just as the pipe was the father of the wind instruments, the
lyre was the father of the stringed instruments. The earliest
ones were the lyre itself, the lute, and the harp.

Because of the rapid ascendency of vocal music, the lyre
came into being as an accompanying instrument. No doubt
it was at first a board or stick over which were stretched a
couple of strings to be twanged with the fingers. Actually,
this first instrument was a lute. The lyre was born when,
back of the strings, a part of the board was cut away. This
left empty space. The strings were tighter, and instead of
being twanged with the fingers, were struck with a piece of
bone or metal.

To clarify the matter, let us say that the lute is the parent
of all instruments whose strings are plucked with the fingers,
and the lyre is the parent of all instruments whose strings
are struck with a plectrum or hammer. Thus, from the lute
came the harp; from the lyre came the dulcimer. The use of
a bow upon strings came much later.

Study the many instruments of a symphony orchestra, and
you will see that there are still just three types, the wind

instruments being subdivided into brasses and woodwinds. Learning the names and characteristics of all the percussion, wind, and stringed instruments is most interesting. Try it!

2. The Bible Record

The role played by instrumental music in Hebrew history was definitely secondary. Their instruments were few, and the drum was not found at all. Nor was there a dulcimer. Even the flute was found rarely, if at all. The lyre, sometimes called a harp, although really not one, was the favorite.

The voice was the thing! To "prophesy" meant to sing. Read Isaiah, in the Hebrew if possible, and learn the truth of this statement. The Hebrews were noted for their lyric poetry and extemporized song. A study of instruments mentioned in the Bible will reveal some strange names; and artists' drawings will reveal shapes just as strange. But no prominent place is given to them. For a detailed study of the musical instruments with accompanying drawings, see *Music in the Bible*.[1]

(1) For the benefit of those who have not made such a study, let us just name and classify them. Under the strings are listed: the *kinnor* (Gen. 4:21); the *nebhel*, which was more harplike, while the former was of the lute type; the *sabeca* (Dan. 3:5–7), very small and having but three or four strings; the *gittith* (Psalms 8, 81, 84); and the kithros or cithara (Dan. 3:5), of the harp or lyre type. All these were light and portable, and some were played as the singer walked.

(2) The wind instruments are also five in number: the *ugab* (Gen. 4:21), a pipe or perhaps two or more pipes; the *halil* (1 Sam. 10:5), a flutelike instrument of reed, wood, bone, or ivory; the *mashrokita* (Dan. 3:5), which was of

---

1. Paul McCommon, *Music in the Bible* (Nashville: Convention Press, 1956), p. 67.

the pipe family; the *shophar* or *keren*, a quite common type of horn, made of a ram's horn or metal; and the *chatsotscrah* (Num. 10:1–10), a straight trumpet.

(3) We have said there were no drums. That is true. There were, however, percussion instruments: the *toph* (Gen. 31:27), or tabret, sometimes called tambourine; the *mesiltayim* (Ezra 3:10); various ringing, tinkling instruments; the *menaanim* (2 Sam. 6:5), similar to our castanets.

II. MUSIC IN OLD TESTAMENT WORSHIP

The Jews seemed to have music for every occasion. Music often became the vehicle for praise, thanksgiving, adoration, or exhortation, regardless of the occasion.

1. *Music in Warfare*

It may be stretching the point somewhat to refer to the use of instruments and voices in warfare as music; but, since the Bible names the instruments used and speaks of the songs of rejoicing, it seems wise to give some space to the subject.

It may be strange to us at first to think of music in warfare as appropriate in a study of music in worship. However, from an early period in Hebrew history, war had a religious significance. In their battles, the warriors were accompanied by their priests. Both campaigns and engagements were opened with sacrificial rites. When the prophets spoke of "preparing" war, they were speaking of religious preparation to sanctify war.

The priests sounded the alarm with trumpets. It was the call to arms. Trumpets were blown also in time of battle to encourage the warriors and remind them that through their God they might gain the victory. At times the trumpet blast was designed to awe and frighten the foe.

When the victors returned from battle, they were met with acclamations and songs of rejoicing (1 Sam. 18:6), and the victory was celebrated with public thanksgiving. For further study, see the use of the trumpet in Leviticus 23:24-25; 25:9; Numbers 10:2 and 31:6.

2. From Adam to David

In Genesis 4:21 we read the record of Jubal, "the father of all such as handle the harp and organ." Abram came from Ur of the Chaldees. Royal tombs there, dated from 3500 to 3200 B.C., gave up to their discoverers several harps and a mosaic showing a woman singing to harp accompaniment.

When Abraham journeyed to Egypt, he found people who were well versed in music. Their instruments were harps, lyres, guitars, mandolins, and single and double flutes. The tabret and harp are mentioned in connection with Jacob and Laban. The use of instruments and song is revealed in Exodus when Moses, Aaron, and Miriam led the people out of Egypt. The voice of the trumpet sounded when Moses went to the mountain to commune with God; also in worship, as revealed in Leviticus 23:24-25 and 25:9.

In the period of the Judges most of the references have to do with war. This has been covered previously. We need only to add the famous song of Deborah and Barak (Judg. 5:1-2).

The last judge was Samuel. We think of him as a prophet rather than a musician. Yet it is said that he belonged to a musical family and that he introduced psalms with musical accompaniment into the services of the tabernacle. He used music to preach righteousness and to uphold morality in a day of decay and demoralization. When he anointed Saul, he told him that he would "meet a company of prophets coming down from the high place with a psaltery, and a tabret, and a pipe, and a harp, before them; and they shall prophesy" (1 Sam. 10:5).

Saul was interested in music during the days of his decline. In his despondency he called again and again for the youthful David to play and sing for him. Music alone seemed to quiet his troubled spirit.

3. *The Temple Chorus and Orchestra*

David was a musician. He played both the harp and the lyre. And he sang! The many psalms attributed to him bear adequate witness. No doubt he possessed great natural talent, but it is evident also that he was trained in the school of the prophets at Ramah, which Samuel had established. Saul said of him: "Behold, I have seen a son of Jesse the Bethlehemite, that is cunning in playing, and a mighty valiant man, and a man of war, and prudent in matters, and a comely person, and the Lord is with him" (1 Sam. 16:18).

After David became king, he made it his business to prepare a tabernacle for the ark of the covenant of the Lord. Masses of people gathered to see the ark removed. Priests, soldiers, Levites, accompanied by players on instruments, and David himself with his harp in his hands, led the procession. There was a choir of four thousand voices and three hundred skilled singers and players upon instruments: Harps, psalteries, cornets, tabrets, and cymbals. Asaph, Heman, and Jeduthun prophesied with harps, psalteries, and cymbals. The sons of these men, divided into twenty-four orders, were later to serve under their fathers.

So David had an elaborate service, but it was his son Solomon who built the great and beautiful Temple and established a service without equal in history. In 2 Chronicles 5:11-12 we read: "And it came to pass, when the priests were come out of the holy place: (for all the priests that were present were sanctified, and did not then wait by course: also the Levites which were the singers, all of them of Asaph, of Heman, of Jeduthun, with their sons and their brethren, being arrayed in white linen, having cymbals and psalteries and harps, stood at the east end of the altar, and with them an hundred and twenty priests sounding with trumpets.)"

There was also a great Passover service in which the pageantry and pomp defy description. Read both 1 and 2 Chronicles in order to receive a full picture of Temple worship.

The days of glory faded. Idolatry invaded the ranks. The people, like the kingdom, were divided. Each king was more evil than his father before him. It was not until the days of Hezekiah and Josiah that worship was restored. In 2 Chronicles 29:25-27 we read: "And he [Hezekiah] set the Levites in the hour of the Lord with cymbals, with psalteries, and with harps, according to the commandment of David, and of Gad the king's seer, and Nathan the prophet: for so was the commandment of the Lord by his prophets. And the Levites stood with the instruments of David, and the priests with the trumpets. And Hezekiah commanded to offer the burnt offering upon the altar. And when the burnt offering began, the song of the Lord began also with the trumpets, and with the instruments ordained by David king of Israel."

It was necessary for Josiah to break down the altars of Baal and re-establish the worship of Jehovah. The Passover was most impressive, and all the Temple services were attended by thousands of people.

In 586 B.C. the people of Judah were carried captive to Babylon. In this fabulous city of wealth and extravagance the worship of heathen gods caused such grief among the people that their songs dried up like streams during a drouth. The experience is given picturesquely by the psalmist in Psalm 137:1-6 RSV:

By the rivers of Babylon,
There we sat down, yea, we wept,
When we remembered Zion.
Upon the willows in the midst thereof
We hanged up our harps.
For there they that led us captive required of us songs,
And they that wasted us required of us mirth, saying,
Sing us one of the songs of Zion.

How shall we sing Jehovah's song
In a foreign land?
If I forget thee, O Jerusalem,
Let my right hand forget her skill.
Let my tongue cleave to the roof of my mouth,
If I remember thee not;
If I prefer not Jerusalem
Above my chief joy.

No doubt some of us, never having suffered such in-dignities, may tend to be critical of those who refused to sing the Lord's songs when a great testimony was needed.

Although another Temple was built, and eventual peace came, the song never returned. The Jews became a down-cast, broken-hearted people. All joy took flight, and they for-bade the use of music and song in their service. Trace the history of Israel down to the present time, and you will find that very little music is used in the orthodox synagogues. The song turned to a wail and a cry that has never died. Never had they been interested in painting, sculpture, or to a large de-gree, architecture. Music was their one art; then it was lost.

III. MUSIC IN NEW TESTAMENT WORSHIP

In the Christian era the persecution of Christians became widespread. Services of corporate worship almost ceased to exist; at their best they were isolated and secret. Through it all, however, music had a significant part, but in a different way. Let us consider these developments.

1. *Paucity of References*

What we have just said in the preceding section may serve as an index to the scanty reference to music in the New Tes-tament. It is quite noticeable that the few existing references have little or nothing to do with music in worship apart from Christian practices. The song was indeed a "new song" im-planted in the hearts of believers.

The birth of Christ was ushered in with music. Angel voices! Heavenly music! How glorious it must have been!

In Luke 1 : 46–55 we have Mary's hymn of praise called the "Magnificat." Be sure to read it. In the same chapter we have the "Benedictus" of Zacharias when the promise of a son (John the Baptist) was fulfilled. When the angels had gone and Jesus was later presented in the Temple, the aged Simeon sang his "Nunc Dimittis" (Luke 2 : 29–32).

Thus we see God's use of joyous music in presenting his Son to the world.

Music, not in worship, but in sorrow and in joy, is revealed in three New Testament accounts. When Jairus' daughter died (Matt. 9 : 23), Jesus found the minstrels making noise. Unless one has heard such Oriental mourning, he cannot imagine how mournful and hair-raising it can be.

In the well-known story of the prodigal son there is reference to the music and dancing at the father's home during the period of rejoicing over the son's return (Luke 15 : 25).

But it was definitely not a singing age. With Rome in the saddle the Jews became a coldhearted, skeptical people, and formalism entered into their service. The promised Messiah came, but the Hebrew people, especially the leaders, did not accept him. There was one time (Mark 11 : 8–10) when the people sang of Jesus. It was at the beginning of his last week. For a brief time the multitudes claimed him as king, singing: "Hosanna; Blessed is he that cometh in the name of the Lord: Blessed be the kingdom of our father David, that cometh in the name of the Lord: Hosanna in the highest."

Doubtless, Jesus sang! His religion of joy and life demanded it. The only reference we have is in the upper room experience at the close of the Last Supper when "they had sung an hymn, they went out into the mount of Olives" (Matt. 26–30). Certainly there is no passage in the story of Jesus that shows he ever condemned singing or the use of musical instruments.

2. Lukan and Pauline Testimony

Luke in Acts and Paul in a few letters open a little window for us. Luke tells of the experience of Paul and Silas (Acts 16) when they were in jail for preaching the Word and for interfering with the use of a young girl for gain. He tells us that they both prayed and sang!

Paul, in writing to the Corinthian Christians, spoke of music being piped or harped (1 Cor. 14:7), using it as an illustration. In verse 8 he emphasizes the need for clean sounding of the trumpet for battle. In the majestic passage on love (1 Cor. 13) he speaks of "sounding brass" and of a "tinkling cymbal."

To the Corinthians, Paul also wrote: "What is it then? I will pray with the spirit, and I will pray with the understanding also: I will sing with the spirit, and I will sing with the understanding also" (1 Cor. 14:15).

The letter to the Colossians contains a rich passage: "Let the word of Christ dwell in you richly in all wisdom; teaching and admonishing one another in psalms and hymns and spiritual songs, singing with grace in your hearts to the Lord" (Col. 3:16).

James in his brief epistle wrote: "Is any among you afflicted? let him pray. Is any merry? let him sing psalms" (James 5:13).

3. New Testament Hymns

What were the songs of New Testament Christians? We have mentioned "psalms and hymns and spiritual songs." Since there were no definitions given, we cannot speak with absolute authority in this area. We can feel, however, that we are on solid ground as we examine the psalms, hymns, and spiritual songs.

(1) *Psalms.*—A psalm is defined as a sacred song or lyric used to celebrate, extol, or praise. The book of Psalms is made

up of 150 such lyrics, many of them attributed to David. These came to be widely used in the worship of Jehovah and continued so into the Christian Era. Because of their expressions of praise, their prayers of supplication, and their wise instructions, they were useful to all who desired to worship the one true and living God.

(2) *Hymns.*—A hymn has been defined as a spiritual meditation, designed, or at least suitable, for singing or chanting in the worship of God. Here is another way of expressing it: A hymn is a song expressive of praise, adoration, or elevated emotion. Specifically, it is a metrical composition divided into stanzas or verses, intended to be sung in religious worship.

(3) *Spiritual songs.*—It is extremely difficult for us to imagine the kind of music to which these early songs were sung. Many writers are sure that the psalms, hymns, and spiritual songs were all crude and shapeless with no meter or form.

With this in mind, let us say that although we do not know how musical these songs were, they ranged from the formal psalm to the exalted hymn to the informal, free, spiritual song. The same degrees are found today in church music. Notice that we do not say these songs ranged up or down. Each person must form his own opinion of the types of music used in and out of the churches.

IV. EARLY CHRISTIAN PRACTICES

The use of music by the early Christians was not the massive, "extravaganza" presentation as evidently employed in Old Testament times. Nevertheless, the contributions made by the early Christians are worth noting. We as singing Christians today owe much to those who preserved and strengthened music in their time.

1. *The Early Christians*

Greek music, it has been said, was born amid the patter of dancing feet, in showers of sunlight, and the swimming of the senses. Although Greek glory had passed, her culture remained, and Rome took up her gay music. Truly she blended all the musics of the pagan world. Originally religious, the music changed in character and moved out to the theaters. Even the plays lost their religious significance.

The chief patron of the new music was the emperor Nero, who was a celebrated professional singer. So seriously did he take his singing that he would practice until late at night and would sleep with plates of lead on his chest to correct unsteadiness of breathing and increase his power and volume of sustained tones.

Nero was an instrumentalist as well, playing the flute, trumpet, and lyre. When the enemy closed in upon him, he went underground and there had a grave prepared. As the noise of the enemy's horses grew louder, he looked into the grave and cried, "What an artist dies in me!" He burst into song. When the song was finished, he set his dagger to his throat and, with the help of his slave, plunged it in.

Pagan music died with him! A new music had begun. Voices could be heard among the tombs and in the catacombs as Christians went through their forbidden worship services. The scholars tell us that their psalms had no meter and no worthy tunes. There was no place for the spirited dance tunes of the Greeks and Romans. We have said that Greek music was born in dancing feet. Christian music was born in subterranean vaults in an atmosphere of terror and darkness with only a feeble ray of hope, despite the fact that congregational singing was prohibited by the Roman church.

There were good days, though few. On the good ones the songs brightened. Three words stood out in their expressions of worship: "alleluia," "amen," and "hosanna." Of course there were others, like "kyrie eleison" on which their voices lingered according to the heart's desire. More than likely their only instrument was the voice. There was little beauty, but abundant meaning.

2. *Gradual Development*

Christianity came out of the tombs. A new day dawned. As the Christians grew stronger and more numerous, they numbered wealthy and influential converts in their ranks and began to worship more openly. Services were held in basilicas and public halls.

Greater freedom resulted in more and better music. Eusebius, quoting Philo said, "Not only do they use the ancient hymns, but they make new ones to God, modulating them in metre and sounds in a very excellent and sweet composition, which is also practiced in the church and in the monasteries."

The name of Clement of Alexandria is the first one found on the list of those who composed hymns in metrical form. He was converted under the leadership of Pananus who was led to Christ by Polycarp, a convert and personal friend of the Apostle John in Ephesus. The oldest hymn now in use, as far as we know, is his "Shepherd of Tender Youth." We quote the first stanza only:

> Shepherd of tender youth
> Guiding in love and truth,
> Through devious ways;
> Christ our triumphant King,
> We come Thy name to sing,
> Hither our children bring
> To shout Thy praise.

Basil the Great, born about one hundred years after Clement's death, put into his own words the "Lamplighting" hymn which he claimed had been in use as early as fifty years after the crucifixion. It is still used in the Greek church. Here is the translation:

> Hail, Jesus Christ, hail, gladdening light
> Of the Immortal Father's glory bright!
> Blessed of all saints beneath the sky,
> And of the heavenly company.

Now, while the sun is setting,
Now, while the light grows dim,
To Father, Son, and Spirit,
We raise our evening hymn.

Worthy Thou while time shall dure,
To be hymned by voices pure;
Son of God, of life the giver,
Thee the world shall praise forever.

Latin hymns played an important part, starting in the fourth century. The first writer of note was Hilary, the father of Western hymnody. This Frenchman prepared the first Christian hymnbook in the Western Church. While in exile, because he provoked the displeasure of the Arian party, he studied the music of the Eastern Church and translated many Greek hymns into Latin. During the same time he also wrote several hymns of his own. Later, he was allowed to return home where he continued his translating and writing.

Ambrose (A.D. 340–97) followed Hilary as musician and poet. He was called "The father of church song." He was made a bishop against his will and became, according to most historians, one of the best bishops who ever guided the religious life of a people.

The music of Ambrose may be described as antiphonal, congregational, and melodious. There is a difference of opinion as to the number of hymns he wrote ranging from twelve to ninety-two. His best known work is:

O Jesus, Lord of heavenly grace,
Thou brightness of Thy Father's face,
Thou fountain of eternal light,
Whose beams disperse the shades of night.

O Christ, with each returning morn
Thine image to our heart be borne,
And may we ever clearly see
Our God and Saviour, Lord, in Thee.

It is claimed that the songs of Ambrose and the prayers of his mother greatly influenced the life of Augustine, leading him from a dissolute and sinful life to salvation and a place in history as one of the world's greatest Christians.

V. THE DARK YEARS

Regardless of how dark and blighted civilization became, the song never entirely disappeared. There were those who cherished music and kept it alive so that people once more would "break forth into singing."

1. *Six Hundred Years*

The Dark Ages are well named. Superstition and ignorance ruled. Society disintegrated. The laboring people were the slaves of the wealthy. Constantine had split the world into the East and the West. Then Roman gates had opened from the inside, and barbarians had swarmed the city. The world trembled at the names of Alaric, Attila, Genseric and the hordes of Goths, Vandals, Franks, Saxons, Danes, Alemanni, Lombards, and Burgundians. Not until the days of modern warfare had the world known such plundering. Civilization was an ash heap. Christianity underwent trying times. How could music live?

2. *One Light Shining*

In all the darkness there was one light. It was the small, flickering light of Christian truth. There were those who seemed to hide that light under the "bushel" of monasticism. Yet it may have been but a shelter to protect the flame like a man cupping his hand around a candlelight against the wind. It was a gesture of retreat. The Christians despaired of saving the barbarian and even their own people. The mountains and the deserts became their homes. With them they took the Scriptures, the hymns, and their piety. Most of monasticism was chaff; but there was some wheat! Out of it all stands the name of Benedict, a man who forsook the world to try to save it. He stopped the retreat of the "holy men" and sent them out to teach, to preach, and to sing!

Charlemagne brought learning out of the monastery and scattered it across the world. The age of missionary endeavor was ushered in. Saint Patrick went from Scotland to Ireland and became "the father of schoolhouses" in northern Europe. Saint Columba went to Scotland and Saint Columban to Gaul. Song went with them wherever they went!

But darkness had the upper hand. A corrupt church. A feudal system. All forsook Christ! All? Not quite. The world had its Theodore, Theophanes, Bernard of Clairvaux, and Bernard of Cluny. Add to these the names of Perotinus Machaut and Dufay, who contributed much to the strengthening and refinement of sacred music during this period. These would not let music die. And with the music there was always a witness for the Saviour.

FOR FURTHER STUDY AND DISCUSSION

1. From the church or public library procure a volume or some volumes on the history of music, and read extensively the material on ancient music and musical instruments.
2. Using this text or *Music in the Bible* (McCommon), list all the musical instruments named in the Bible. Then use a concordance to locate each and read about it in its context.
3. Again with your concordance, look up the words "song," "singing," etc., and read about the use of vocal music in the Bible. If you do not have a large concordance, go to your church library or your pastor's study for help.
4. Memorize Psalms 1, 23, and 100. Read again and again (memorize if possible) the "magnificat" of Mary (Luke 1:46–55).

CHAPTER 3 OUTLINE

I. REFORMATION HYMNS

II. ENGLISH HYMNODY

III. AMERICA'S PART

IV. MUSIC WITHOUT WORDS

V. WORDS AND MUSIC

Church Music from the Sixteenth to the Twentieth Century

CONCEPTIONS OF MUSIC and attitudes toward it and its relationship to worship vary greatly. These variations of concepts and opinions have existed for generations and perhaps will always exist. Its use as a means of worship, regardless of the application or methodology, is almost as old as time itself. However, the developments perhaps most significant to today's worshiper started with the Reformation period.

Beginning with the Reformation and continuing to the present time, the contributions to music and worship have been consistent and progressive. In a sense, those who worship today join hands with Luther and all the intermediary contributors to this great cause. Each generation has made its contribution. In each instance, the worthy has been retained and the impractical eliminated. We are the recipients! Let us consider some of the developments.

I. REFORMATION HYMNS

During the Dark Ages there arose an ever-increasing number of hymns to the virgin Mary, to the apostles, and to certain saints. Other hymns were meditations on the passion and the wounds of Christ, the joys of paradise, and the terrors of the judgment. The fourteenth century saw a marked increase in reverence to the "blessed virgin" and a decrease in reverence to the risen Lord. Among the books that came from this period were the *Psalter of Mary, Marian Litany*, the *Garland of Salutations, Rosaries of Mary,* and *The Prayers to the Praises of Mary.*

1. *Luther's Influence*

Perhaps the two greatest influences, other than the men who led the way, were the renewed interest in the Bible and the spread of sacred melody. One of Martin Luther's first moves was to find people who could compose hymns and spiritual songs. He was personally responsible for the Reformation marching song, "A Mighty Fortress Is Our God." He was from childhood a lover of music, and early in life he recognized its persuasive power. Critics of the great reformer claimed that he was singing people into the Lutheran doctrine, and that he was destroying more souls with his singing than with his writing and preaching.

When Luther realized that his movement demanded careful planning and organization, he urged two choirmasters to make their home with him. They consented to do so, and while with him they wrote a liturgy for the Reformed Church. Four printers in Erfurt were kept busy publishing his hymns and compilations. Many of them were not original, but were based on the psalms, other Scripture passages, the catechism, and old Latin and German hymns. Therefore, it is difficult to determine just how many original hymns he actually wrote. Julian's *Dictionary of Hymnology states*: "Of Luther's hymns no classification can be quite perfect." They were, however, strictly evangelical and were adapted to the use of a congregation in public worship. Many of the selections used by Luther were folk tunes and melodies long familiar to the people. He reasoned that a familiarity with the tune would aid greatly in their learning and singing the hymn.

Paul Gerhardt, born March 12, 1607, was second only to Luther as a gifted and popular hymn writer. He prepared for the ministry, but no pulpit was immediately open to him. Because he was well educated, he became a tutor in Berlin.

He fell in love with his pupil and married her. Not long before that he had been ordained a Lutheran minister and had become a pastor at Mittenwalde. Later he was called to a church in Berlin where he became quite successful. He published a number of hymns which soon became widely known and used throughout Germany.

Gerhardt was faithful to his task, and his faithfulness resulted in opposition. He was removed from his office, restored, and then removed again. Death came to his son, and soon thereafter to his wife. But he remained faithful to the end. Under his portrait, which hangs in the church he served, is the inscription: "A divine, sifted in Satan's sieve."

The pattern was set. The movement sang its way onward. Count von Zinzendorf, restorer of the Moravians, a small missionary organization, married a gifted hymn writer and became both preacher and hymn writer during the tempestuous days in the middle of the eighteenth century. For many years he was exiled from his homeland because of charges of heresy. During these years he traveled in other countries, visiting Christian workers. On his return, he resumed his writing as well as his preaching. More than two thousand hymns are credited to him.

It is said that Germany has had, throughout the centuries, the best mass singing of all countries. The people liked to sing. They had the best music available. In no other country has the chorale been so popular or so well sung.

2. *In France*

Clovis was king of the Franks. He was a heathen, his wife a Christian. When a battle was going the wrong way, in desperation he prayed to his wife's God. In his prayer he promised that if his army returned victorious he would turn from his idolatry and embrace Christianity. The tide turned. Victory came. Clovis made a profession of faith in Christ. His method of "converting" his people could hardly be called evangelistic, but Christianity became the accepted religion at his court.

The ruler was greatly interested in music. He sent to Italy for a musician. Then, upon his arrival, he gave him full sway in developing vocalists and instrumentalists.

The first hymns to be used were French translations of ancient Latin hymns. Roman Catholic hymns, written to popular ballad tunes, were added. Later there was the development of carols, Scripture narratives, and hymns. Tunes from operas were often used.

The French Reformation brought to the front the people called Huguenots. No other Protestant group suffered more indignities. Their hymn writers were thrown into prison. Many were drowned in the Seine River. Naked bodies were piled in the streets. In the prisons, in the galleys, in dungeons, and in battle, the Huguenots sang psalms. Godly men wrote moving, Scripture-filled songs. Jannequin, Bourgeois, Louis, Goudimel, Le Jeune, and others wrote the music. Highly trained choirs sang songs written for three, five, even six parts.

Claude Goudimel was outstanding among the writers of music. Palestrina, "the father of religious music" was his pupil. Goudimel heads the list of Huguenots who died in a fanatical massacre in Lyons. Why was he killed? Not for preaching, but for setting psalms to music!

Time and space do not permit the extolling of the virtues of Clement Marot and Theodore de Beze. France has added glorious chapters to the history of sacred music.

II. ENGLISH HYMNODY

The English people did not have a Luther, as did the Germans, to lead out in introducing hymn singing to all the people. Neither was it easy for the English to depart from the practice of singing Latin praises, nor later from the well established practice of singing the psalms. Many conditions influenced these developments. Let us consider some of the most important.

1. *From Psalm to Hymn*

In England there was a development from the psalm to the hymn against the protest of the Roman Church. In fact the people had been forbidden to take part in singing, no doubt because of the influence of mass singing in Germany. In 1549 Robert Crowley versified the whole psalter in common meter (C.M.) and set it to a harmonized chant. A real singing movement was about to be set in motion when Mary came to the throne. Under her rule people were not allowed to sing psalms. Despite her power, psalm singing gained ground among exiled Christians, for many of them were to be found in the vicinity of Geneva, and they came under the influence of John Calvin and his psalm singing.

2. *The Early Period (1623—1700)*

When Mary died and Elizabeth came to the throne another change took place. Elizabeth loved music! She not only permitted the use of psalms, but allowed an expansion into the field of hymn singing. The first hymnbook was published in 1623, titled *Songs of the Church*. The volume contained no music. The tunes were indicated at the head of each song. George Wither was the publisher.

It was during this period, due much to the encouragement of Queen Elizabeth, that William Byrd and Thomas Tallis exerted tremendous influence on music. Their influence extended not only to the composing of music, but also to the techniques of publishing it.

In 1647 Herrick's *Noble Numbers* was published. It contained songs for special occasions such as Christmas and the New Year. Other books appeared every few years in the Church of England, but approximately seventeen hundred hymns were also introduced into the nonconformist's worship. The Baptists under the leadership of Benjamin Keach were the first to adopt them. Persecution, as usual, followed. Once he was trampled under the hoof of troopers' horses; once he was thrown into prison. Even in his own church there was a division over singing. Two bodies were formed: the singing and the nonsinging. In 1691 Keach wrote a book in defense of singing in worship. The book title was *The Breach Repaired*. Not all Baptists were converted by his strong leadership and his book, but he did win the victory among his own congregation. In 1691 he published a volume of three hundred hymns titled *Spiritual Melody*. This was followed by his *Spiritual Songs* in 1696.

3. *The Later Period (1700—1887)*

Minds were now more receptive. Men praised God in song. Thanks to Isaac Watts and John and Charles Wesley, a new day dawned for music in worship. Watts's first volume was made up of both hymns and psalms. At least seven books came from his pen from 1706 to 1737. Among them were *Hymns and Spiritual Songs for the Use of Children,* and *The Psalms of David*. In addition to his hymns he published hundreds of sermons. Perhaps Watts's most important contribution to, and influence on, congregational singing was that he made a Christianized version of the psalms, thus paving the way for hymns of human composure.

It was in 1738 that the first volume came from the pen of John Wesley. It contained seventy hymns. It is interesting to note that the book was divided into three parts: *Psalms and Hymns for Sundays, Psalms and Hymns for Wednesdays and Fridays,* and *Psalms and Hymns for Saturdays*. Not all of the hymns were written by John. Isaac Watts, other members of the Wesley family, and still other writers contributed to the collection.

Later there were volumes by John and Charles together. They wrote hymns by the hundreds. Many of them are favorites today. Other men compiled hymnbooks, using the writings of Watts and the Wesleys, often altering them and incurring the disfavor of their authors.

Throughout this period, hymn writing continued at an amazing pace. At least two volumes each year for twenty years came off the press. In 1833 ten volumes were published in twelve months.

In England, especially in the Church of England, church music has been held on a very high level. Never have the English people succumbed to mercenary songbook publishers. However, as is true in America, the use of the gospel song has been important in evangelism and has kept the service of worship from becoming too stilted.

The music of the Church of England is designed for the orderly, stately services of cathedrals. Nonconforming music is designed for the Sunday schools, revival meetings, missions, and churches dotting the rural and village areas. Both types of music are making a real contribution. Each has its place.

4. *The Writers*

The hymnbooks in England reached back into ancient times for much of their literature and added it to the prolific works of Watts, Wesley, and others. This fact is evidenced by a hymnal published in 1931 by the Church of England, titled *The English Hymnal*. Material for it came from Latin, Greek, German, Swiss, French, American, Italian, and Spanish, as well as English, sources. Starting with Ambrose the list of hymn writers includes St. Thomas Aguinas, Bernard of Clairvaux, Bernard of Cluny, Fortunatas, Gregory the Great, Bede, Justinian, Luther, Savier, Palestrina, Bourgeois, Cruger, Bach, Montgomery, Cowper, Watts, Toplady, Kipling, Longfellow, Lowell, Holmes, Wesley, Fanny Crosby, Doane, Mason, and Sankey.

The nonconformists, using *Alexander's Hymns No. 3* and

others, chose hymns by Sir Arthur Sullivan, Sir Joseph Barnby, Gauntlett, Mendelssohn, Dykes, Monk, McGranahan, Harkness, Towner, Gabriel, Stebbins, Excell, Lorenz, Bliss, Doane, Ackley, and Morris. Most of these are well known in America. Check the index of composers in your *Baptist Hymnal* or other hymnals, and see how many of these you recognize.

5. *Their Hymns*

To see how we in America have drawn upon the same sources, we shall list many of the best-known hymns from these same two books.

In the *English Hymnal* we find "Fling Out the Banner," "Just As I Am," "My Faith Looks Up to Thee," "O Day of Rest and Gladness," "O Jesus, I Have Promised," "Onward, Christian Soldiers," "Rock of Ages," "Safe in the Arms of Jesus," "Take My Life, and Let It Be," "Tell Me the Old, Old Story," and "Love Divine, All Loves Excelling." How England and America have combined their talents!

Among the hymns and choruses in *Alexander's Hymns No. 3* are the familiar "Crown Him with Many Crowns," "Sun of My Soul," "Abide with Me," "The Banner of the Cross," "He Will Hold Me Fast," "The Fight Is On," "Hallelujah for the Cross," "Remember Me, O Mighty One," "Nearer, Still Nearer," "Send a Revival," "Praise Him!" "Jesus Bids Us Shine," and "The Little Lord Jesus."

Again let us check our hymnals and become familiar with each of these songs.

III. AMERICA'S PART

It is difficult for us to realize the changes that have taken place in church music in this country since Colonial days. Let us take a brief look at some of the interesting developments.

1. *The Pilgrims and the Puritans*

It is easy for us to confuse the Puritans with the pilgrims. The Puritans were a sect of English Protestants in the sixteenth century who advocated popular rights and opposed ritualism and laxity of morals. They were among the pilgrim settlers of New England.

The pilgrims, usually called Pilgrim Fathers, were English colonists who settled Plymouth, Massachusetts, in 1620. The name was derived from the word which means wanderer or wayfarer, one who journeys, especially on foot, to some sacred place, for religious purposes. The Pilgrim Fathers were a persecuted people who fled first to Holland, where they could worship God according to their own consciences, and later to America. Let it be clear, then, that all who anchored off Cape Cod December 9, 1620, were pilgrims; but not all were Puritans. The Puritans held views established by the Church of England, but the pilgrims held independent views.

Song played a very important part in the movement. The preacher and scholar, Henry Ainsworth, was not only a champion for the cause of religious freedom, but also a prolific writer of hymns. As the people were preparing to leave for America, they met at their pastor's home and sang psalms. Their singing also brought comfort to their souls on the journey across the Atlantic. Bible reading and singing filled the long, tedious hours.

When the *Mayflower* landed, the women stayed on board while the men went ashore. There they worshiped God with prayers and psalm singing. They used Ainsworth's book, an English publication, which had been published in 1612. It was called *The Book of Psalms*. It was replaced in 1640 by the famous *Bay Psalm Book*. The first music in American churches was psalm singing, and *Bay Psalm Book* was the first American psalmbook.

How interesting it would be if we could somehow sit in on one of their services. They paid no attention at all to rhythm. They sang no parts. For fear of imitating the papists they used no notes. The singing had to be slow and monotonous because lively music was "of the devil." One writer, in an article about singing, claimed that he often paused twice on one note to take a breath. Sometimes thirty minutes was required for the singing of one psalm. Their older book had five tunes; the newer one six! There were no choirs. All the people sang. And they found satisfaction in their singing.

2. *The Gradual Change*

Singing societies were formed about 1720 and, for the first time, psalms were used in a paraphrased form. Oh, there was opposition. Always a change brings opposition. But it established a trend which resulted in the use of more and more freedom which was popular with the masses.

The first Baptist hymnal was issued in 1766. A collection from various authors, it was called *Hymns and Spiritual Songs*. It opened with sixteen hymns on baptism. The works of Watts and Wesley greatly influenced the Baptists.

The early Baptist groups were highly emotional and chose the songs that would fit the mood of the service. Other denominations as well as Baptists often had differing opinions concerning music. Hisses and jeers sometimes came from the congregations. Ministers had to leave their pulpits.

The coming of the camp meeting in 1800 brought about the most marked change in singing practices. Hundreds flocked to the services. There were no songbooks to fit their needs; so the hymns were "lined out" from the pulpit, and the music flowed from the hearts of the people. The appeal was directed to sinners, backsliders, and mourners. Songs of emotion were in demand. The new movement was significant in that it ushered into use some of the truly great songs, such as "When I Survey the Wondrous Cross," "There Is a

Fountain," "Work for the Night Is Coming," "Amazing Grace," and others.

3. *America's Hymn Writers*

Lowell Mason is called the father of American church music. How fortunate that there was a man of such talent and training. It was he who founded the Boston Academy of Music; who became president and conductor of the Handel and Haydn Society. Because he desired to reach the masses, he introduced music into the public schools. So anxious was he to spread the gospel of good music that in 1851 he went to other cities organizing, directing, promoting it. He joined with Thomas Hastings who helped publish several books which became very popular.

In 1842 *The Baptist Hymn Book* was published by W. C. Buck in Louisville, Kentucky. This was but the beginning. Robert Lowry took up the crusade. Dwight L. Moody popularized the gospel song, having as his helper the talented, fervent Ira D. Sankey. Philip P. Bliss, George C. Stebbins, Fanny J. Crosby, W. H. Doane, E. O. Excell, Charles H. Gabriel, and Robert Harkness were only a few who added immeasurably to the crusade for good music in worship. Among those who excelled in the writing of songs for evangelism were Gabriel and Harkness.

IV. MUSIC WITHOUT WORDS

Earlier in this book we studied the ancient musical instruments. During the centuries we have just covered, the voice was used almost exclusively in worship. However, instruments were used in some countries, especially in the art and entertainment fields.

1. *The Orchestra*

Not many churches use the orchestra regularly for worship services. A few churches use small orchestral groups in Sunday school and even in church worship services, but the large orchestra is more frequently used to accompany singers in great oratorios and cantatas.

The modern symphony orchestra is made up of instruments which have come from many lands. All can be placed in one of the classifications listed in the second chapter: percussion, wind (brass and woodwind), and stringed.

It was not until the seventeenth century that orchestras, as we know them today, were formed. Monteverdi led the way. There are sources that cite his scoring of the opera, *Orfeo*, as the approximate beginning of the modern orchestra. It was vitally necessary to accompany the singers in the great dramas that were being produced in Italy and Germany. Therefore, opera and the orchestra developed somewhat side by side over a period of years. While not used in worship, many of the greatest productions had a strong religious significance.

So pleased were the musicians with the accomplishments of the orchestra as an accompanying group that more and more "music without words" came into being. Now the output of music without words may have surpassed that with words. America, at last, is taking the orchestra and its music seriously.

2. *The Organ*

Here again we consider an accompanying instrument. The organ is a veritable orchestra at the finger tips of one person. Technically however, the organ should not be classified as a "one-man" orchestra, for it is an instrument that is distinctive in itself. Only the romantics corrupted it to imitate the orchestra; the contemporary classic organ is a much better worship instrument than its romantic counterpart. It was born a Panpipe in a remote period. The syrinx, or hydraulic organ, was invented about 200 B.C. Wind was pumped into a chest and forced into the pipes. Later a bagpipe was used. Additional inventions and improvements came periodically. For an interesting history of the instrument, read the article on organ in the *Encyclopaedia Brittanica.*

Organ building on a large scale began in England in the tenth century. How different the instrument is today. The principle is the same, but every part has been modernized and improved.

We have called the organ an accompanying instrument. And so it is. But it is also a solo instrument without equal. No words are needed. The full gamut of emotions may be run by a truly great organist on a truly great instrument.

The "king of instruments" is the pipe organ. There are some excellent electric organs, but not one can take the place of the king.

3. *The Piano*

The organ was the first keyed instrument. The next was the clavichord, which dates back to the fifteenth century. If we include the Pythagorean monochord, we must move back to the eleventh century. The clavichord gave way to the harpsichord, the harpsichord to the pianoforte in the eighteenth century. The pianola, or player piano, flourished for a while and died. The piano remains as possibly our most popular instrument, being widely used as an instrument for accompaniment and also as a solo instrument.

The organ came into the churches with comparative ease. Not so the piano! Battles were fought, churches were split. The piano won the victory. Today, in most churches where both organ and piano are used, the latter occupies space equal to that of the console.

4. *Other Instruments*

In many of the churches today some smaller solo instruments are used. However, there are some churches that refuse to admit them. Of these, the most acceptable is the violin. It is a beautiful solo instrument when skilfully played. Its sound is frightful when poorly played! Some churches use a harp, a cello, or a marimba on occasions. The trombone and the trumpet enter with the dynamic song leader for revivals. Just what place these instruments have had in centuries past we do not know.

It is known, however, that in the time of Buxtehude (died 1707), strings, reeds, and brass instruments were used frequently to accompany the music in churches. They complemented the limited organ of that day. Trumpets and trombones were used by the Germans in Reformation times, and G. Gabrieli used them in sacred music at St. Mark's, Venice, around 1600. Brass instruments have played a large part in the festivals of evangelical churches throughout the centuries.

V. WORDS AND MUSIC

Very briefly we shall consider the use of words and music in worship since A.D. 1500. We have dealt adequately with the psalm, the hymn, and the gospel song. No space has been given to the remaining forms: the chant, mass, chorale, anthem, oratorio, and music drama.

1. *The Chant*

A chant is a melody repeated with the several verses of a prose text, a number of syllables being intoned on each reciting note.

Use of the chant dates back to a very early period. It was introduced under the direction of St. Ambrose (A.D. 340–97) and Pope Gregory (A.D. 540–604), both of whom supervised the collecting and compiling of chants for use by the church.

In the Catholic Church the chant refers to the singing of psalms, canticles, etc., in plainsong, to Latin words. In the Anglican Church it refers to the singing of psalms to harmonized and measured tunes. However, with the Anglican usage, the rhythm is often modified or obscured because of the necessity of fitting in the longer or shorter psalm verses. Some modern hymnals include a few chants, but they are rarely used by Baptist churches.

2. *The Mass*

The "Mass" is the name for the chief ritual of the Roman Catholic Church in the observance of the Eucharist. Starting as early as the fourteenth century, the Mass was set to music and has continued to be treated as a form of musical composition. The early masses were polyphonic in treatment. The chanting style is used ordinarily with the priests, choirs, and congregation participating. However, instrumental masses and symphonic masses were written by Mozart, Haydn, Schubert, Beethoven, Verdi, and others. Those works were magnificent—operatic in style and not particularly religious. These removed participation from the congregation even as the oratorio or cantata does in our churches. Some of the more elaborate masses of the eighteenth and nineteenth centuries are used today for concert purposes.

The requiem Mass for the dead produced special musical forms and brought out some of the greatest art of the masters named above.

3. *The Chorale*

The German reformers gave us the chorale. Actually, "chorale" is the German word for "hymn." They took the chant, used some features of it, embellished it, and produced the new art form, the chorale. Luther, Walther, Bach, and others contributed to the new form, giving us many newly composed chorales. Although this form never became as popular in other countries as in Germany, it was used in England, France, and North America. Choral societies were formed. Great choirs flourished. Another important step was taken in providing worshipful music for the churches.

4. *The Anthem*

The anthem, though derived from the Greek language, originated with the Church of England. In the order of service it always had the same place, immediately following the "third collect," both morning and evening. Sometimes a hymn was used at that time, even as today. Ordinarily, however, a more elaborate composition, the anthem, is sung by the choir. Most often it is set to words from the Bible, but there seems to be a trend away from that type of anthem. Many anthems feature solo parts, although there is also an increasing departure from this practice.

The anthem in the Church of England was comparable to the motet used in Roman Catholic and Lutheran churches. The outstanding composers of anthems in the sixteenth century were Tallis, Tye, Byrd, and Farrant; in the seventeenth century Orlando Gibbons, Blow, and Purcell; in the eighteenth, Croft, Boyce, Kent, Nares, Cooke, and Arnold.

5. *The Music Drama*

The next progressive change in musical composition was directed toward a new form known as the music drama. In the secular field it became known as the opera. In the religious, the oratorio. No exact date can be established as the beginning of opera, although it did come into use in the early part of the seventeenth century. Monteverdi's pupil, Cavalli, along with Cesti, Stradella, and others were among the early composers of opera. The names of Monteverdi, Steffani, Lully, Rameau, Handel, Gluck, Mozart, Verdi, and others are significant in establishing opera as a permanent music form.

The opera is a musical work for stage of varying types. Operas are usually staged, but not always. The oratorio is a vocal work usually for solo voices and chorus, with some kind of instrumental accompaniment, and usually treating a subject of sacred character. The cantata is an extended vocal work, consisting of chorus and solos, occasionally recitatives, duets, etc., with instrumental accompaniment. The cantata is usually distinguished from oratorio or opera by the exclusion of scenic effects and the dramatic element.

Oratorios are ordinarily given in concert. The cantata which is not as heavy or as long as the oratorio is also given, usually, in concert. In the churches where space and talent combine to make it possible, both oratorios and cantatas have been presented in costume, often with much of the brilliance of operatic staging.

Bach and Handel are to the oratorio what Verdi and Wagner are to the opera. Music drama has a place, a very great place in the music world and in the Christian world.

FOR FURTHER STUDY AND DISCUSSION

1. In order to understand the part music played in the Reformation, it is necessary to know the history of that period. Ask your librarian for a book on the Reformation and read the story of the major events and the lives of the greatest men.
2. There are many hymns listed in this chapter. Take your *Baptist Hymnal, Broadman Hymnal, Modern Hymnal,* or other good standard works, and look up each hymn. Read the hymn carefully to find its message. If possible, play the hymn tune or have it played.
3. Make a list of all instruments used in a large symphony orchestra, arranging them according to the classifications given in chapter 2.
4. Study your church organ. Learn from the organist the meaning of the words on the knobs and tabs.

CHAPTER 4 OUTLINE

I. THE SCOPE OF THE FIELD

II. THE GROWING DEMAND

III. MAKING THE MOST OF EACH SERVICE

IV. THE PSYCHOLOGY OF ATTENTION

4

Music in Worship Services Today

TRULY, we live in the day of churches. Southern Baptists alone have more than 32,000 churches in the rural areas, villages, towns, and cities. In most of them, as well as churches of other denominations, music has been a vital part of the programs and the worship services. The heavy accent on music in the public schools, as well as in the entertainment field, has resulted in a greater music interest in most of the churches. Having delved into past centuries for a glimpse of music in worship, we are now ready to look into present-day practices and problems.

The time was when there was little help and guidance available for churches. Furthermore, there was a scarcity of materials suited to Baptist churches and the type of program we seek to promote.

That condition is rapidly changing. There has been a phenomenal upsurge of interest in music. Denominational leaders have responded to the need, and as a result Southern Baptists now have a program of music training and improvement that is planned for every church, regardless of size or location. This program will enable churches without an organized Music Ministry to have one. It enables churches which already have a Music Ministry to have a better one.

Materials and helps, as well as trained personnel to assist in training necessary leadership and implementing an effective Music Ministry are available at state and associational levels. Churches need only to request help in behalf of a more effective Music Ministry.

I. The Scope of the Field

Southern Baptist churches vary greatly, both in size, and in location. However, one basic principle can be established at this point: Any church, regardless of its size or location, can utilize music as an effective and sincere expression of worship.

1. *The Open Country Church*

Among Baptists, open country churches predominate. Most of them are small. Some still have quarter-time or half-time preaching. There is no such thing as a church "staff" among them. In most cases the pastor is the only salaried worker.

Of course this means that much will depend on the pastor. Often trained song leaders are not available. In most instances qualified pianists can be enlisted, but qualified organists are rare. Adults, youth, and children are interested in belonging to a choir. They have the interest and ability but lack the essential skills. If the pastor has had sufficient training, it is sometimes necessary for him to assume some of the leadership responsibility. Usually he must take the initiative in enlisting potential leaders and then give them encouragement and guidance in acquiring the necessary training.

The greatest need has been for leadership, for usually there is some available talent. A small membership usually means small choirs. A small membership may rule out a fully graded choir program; however, there is always a strong possibility that a church with a graded education program can have at least a partially graded choir program. When there are talented volunteer leaders, such a program can usually be developed.

As a result of the helps and materials that are now available through various denominational channels, many of the smaller churches that once had little more than congregational singing, and occasionally "special music" from the hymnal by a small, unrehearsed choir, now have several choirs, trained volunteer leaders, and a Music Ministry in general that would put some larger churches to shame. In many cases, these choirs at first had no regular rehearsals except for a Christmas program or some other special event. Now they have regularly scheduled rehearsals as a part of the church calendar of activities.

Unfortunately, the move to the larger towns and cities has robbed the open country church of some of its strength, and in some instances there is a dearth of young people, both single and married. In some areas, however, the open country churches are experiencing a remarkable growth and reactivation. The denominational zeal in the interest of the open country church is unparalleled in our denominational history. As towns have expanded, some open country churches have been brought within the fringe of the town. Some small churches have followed the example of consolidated schools and have used buses to good advantage.

The rural areas were at one time the last to benefit from new developments and advancements, but that situation also has changed. The public school, good roads, and better communication have entered the picture. The consolidated schools have in many instances matched music programs with the best of the larger towns and cities. In so doing, they have not only enlarged the vision of the people, but have aided in training and developing talent that can be utilized in the open country churches. The music in many of these churches started to develop when they began to take full advantage of the training given its young people in the public schools!

No, the future is not dark. Better-trained pastors, more experienced lay members, television and radio programs which enable the people to hear (and see) fine choral, as well as instrumental groups, plus recordings and other media, have helped to lift the level of music appreciation in many churches. The denominational music program has "majored" on music training at the associational and local church levels, and the open country churches have benefited greatly. Many of the helps are planned specifically for the improvement of music and its varied uses in worship activities.

2. *The Village Church*

A step above the open country church in size and in potential strength is the village or town church. We must realize that there are churches both small and large in towns as well as in metropolitan areas. For convenience we shall think of the village church as the church of medium size with its location in a town of medium, or even small, population.

With this consideration we are thinking of literally thousands of churches which are perhaps most representative of a large segment of our denomination. Many of the ministers are trained. Many of these churches have a staff, in addition to the pastor. There often is a church secretary who serves on a full-time schedule, a "combination" man who directs both the music and education program, and a custodian. Here the organist or pianist or possibly both may be employed by the church on a part-time basis, or they may serve entirely as volunteer workers.

The majority of these churches can be considered under one heading because of the basic similarity in the "music in worship" part of the church service. It is in these churches that the quest for better music, along with a more effective use of it as a medium of worship, has experienced an almost phenomenal growth. Exceptions will be pointed out as we proceed.

Almost without exception, these churches have the following things in common in the music of the worship service: organ and/or piano preludes, offertories, postludes, and accompaniments; choral responses, anthems, solos (vocal and instrumental); congregational singing. In general, the equipment is not as adequate, the programs as fully developed, or the talent as plentiful as is found in the large city churches, but there is certainly no less warmth and no less appreciation on the part of the people. The same hymnals are used. Many of the same anthems stock the shelves of the music library.

Since the village or town church is so representative of Southern Baptist constituency, what has already been achieved in these churches, musically speaking as well as in other areas of development and progress, may well be used both as a standard and criterion for progress. They have proved over and over that an effective Music Ministry is within the reach of practically every church.

3. The "Big Church"

Having dealt with the open country and town churches, it is natural to think of the city church. But the whole picture has changed in the cities. There are far more small churches than large. New churches are springing up in every area of city expansion. Most of these have "city ways," but their size and financial strength limit them severely. Therefore, we have used the word "big" in referring to churches whose membership numbers in the thousands rather than in the hundreds.

The large church has almost unlimited talent and often sufficient funds to do whatever the program demands. Both organ and piano are used in the worship services. Often a violinist plays regularly with the other instrumentalists and sometimes plays offertory solos. Some few churches have an organist-director, but most of them employ a minister of music who directs the entire music program.

In these churches music plays a major part. Not only the size of the congregation, but the strong leadership of a great choir and powerful instruments help make congregational singing above the average. Worship services are usually well planned, church bulletins are attractively printed, and the work of the choir shows that adequate preparation has been made through well-planned rehearsals. A word of caution, however, must be added at this point. Not *all* large churches have a Music Ministry that meets the highest standards, nor do they always achieve their maximum possibilities in this area. Many do, but there are numerous instances in which churches much smaller in size and potential have made greater strides in the establishment and use of a Music Ministry. Large churches also often need guidance in this area.

Because of the size and quality of the choirs in the large churches, more difficult anthems are sung, and cantatas and oratorios are well spaced throughout the year.

Thus, we have the churches, large and small, and all sizes in between, challenging Baptist music leaders to give the best counsel, prepare the finest materials, and provide the best leadership possible. The scope of the field is wide. The task is great.

II. The Growing Demand

We have pointed out the growing demand in the previous section. In order to emphasize it we shall now consider leadership, graded choirs, instruments, accompanists, and equipment. Let us keep in mind that at present we are dealing with the survey of the music field in churches today. We shall make a more detailed study of these same subjects later, using a different approach.

1. *Demand for Leadership*

The word "demand" is used deliberately. People travel and visit extensively; they see worship services on television and hear them on the radio. They are aware of modern trends.

They know immediately how their own churches compare with the others they touch. Thus, there is a resultant demand for better music in the local church.

Most persons are aware of the leadership problem. They are also aware of problems in the other areas of church work. In some instances, the pastor has to "sell" the people on the worth of a new staff member, most notably perhaps, an assistant to the pastor or a youth director. Occasionally, the people are first to see the need and find it necessary to convince the pastor.

One of the first things experienced in the large churches was the necessity for the employment of a full-time minister of music. The combination of music and education has always been a child of necessity rather than a desirable arrangement. No matter how skilled one may be in both fields, the vast difference in them makes the correlation of the work most difficult. Wherever possible, the churches are employing a full-time music leader. In some of the larger churches, one occasionally finds a music staff consisting of the minister of music, organist (and/or pianist), and music secretary. Other part-time workers are used with the graded choirs.

2. Call for Graded Choirs

People of all ages like to sing; need to sing! The Sunday school and the Training Union have place for a great deal of singing, but no place for music training. Too often children are not considered in planning a worship service. The growing demand for better church music several years ago reached into the elementary and youth departments. The old booster band was not the answer.

Today the expanding program of graded choirs is appealing to all adults, especially young parents. Children are really learning music! They know some theory. They respond to well-organized activity.

The call came. Then came the answer. The future is bright in church music. High standards have been set, and with eagerness all age groups are reaching toward them.

3. *Better Instruments Required*

Many can recall the days when the only good piano in the building was in the auditorium where the worship services were held. All others were gifts from members who wanted to rid themselves of an old instrument, especially an old player piano. The trend today is toward new pianos just the right size for the department assembly room. Many are even finished to match the color scheme of the room. Grand pianos are in use almost everywhere for church worship services.

The electric organ has become very popular among the churches which are financially unable to purchase pipe organs. There is now a wide price range for these instruments varying from approximately a thousand dollars to several thousands. The pipe organ is still the most desirable instrument. Its field begins with two ranks unified and runs up to one hundred or more ranks.

Not only is there a demand for better instruments, but the upkeep of organs and pianos is an accepted item in church budgets. Two tunings each year are highly desirable.

4. *The Quest for Accompanists*

Naturally, an increased interest in music in worship has led, in all the churches, to an urgent demand for capable accompanists. More churches are removing rigid restrictions pertaining to the organ and are allowing students to use it for lessons and practice. In some places the Music Ministry provides piano classes as a part of the church program. Thus, persons who had once played the piano have a refresher course, and others who had never studied the instrument learn enough to serve as helpers in elementary and youth departments. Here, too, we are indebted to the increased emphasis on music in the public schools.

5. *The Demand for Equipment*

A definite part of the upward trend in music in worship today has been the demand for better equipment. Churches want the best hymnals for use in worship. Southern Baptists made available one of the finest in recent years with the publication of *Baptist Hymnal* in 1956.

Choir robes are used in more and more churches. And they are more beautiful than ever. Colors are chosen with care. They are sent to the cleaners more often. What the people request in our churches they eventually receive!

Money is wisely spent on good public address systems, tape recorders, record players, and other equipment so vitally necessary in teaching and training. Every step is designed to assist man in worshiping and honoring God.

III. Making the Most of Each Service

There is no compulsion that will impel people to attend worship services except the compulsion of desire. If the service becomes uninteresting, the attendance record will hold up for a while because of habit or a sense of duty, but then the break will come. The desire is gone.

1. *Planned Services Necessary*

In many churches, modern worship services reflect wise planning. In others, it is noticeably absent. Regardless of size of the church, serious planning should go into each service. The church bulletin is commonly used, even in the small church today. But its use does not always indicate careful planning. A study of bulletins will show that too often the order of service has been set without a variation, except for the hymn numbers and other musical notations, and has remained unchanged for years. We recall one bulletin that has come to the desk weekly for fifteen years and the one line in the bulletin for both morning and evening services has remained "Sermon. . . . .Pastor." Never has a subject been listed! No, in this instance the use of a bulletin proves little.

The actual planning will come later in this study, but it must be pointed out here that slipshod, haphazard worship services dishonor God! He is worthy of the best music, the best preaching, the most humble devotion of which we are capable.

2. The Need for Balance

A careful study of worship services in many different churches has revealed a real need for proper balance. By the term "balance" we mean a service with every part having the time needed for giving attention to the spiritual diet of the worshiper.

In one church the sermon is the part that destroys the balance. In another it is the music. In still another, strange to say, it is the making of announcements. Later the matter of balance will be studied in detail. Just now our purpose is to show that in worship services today, generally there is not enough balance. There must be something vital and challenging for each person in the congregation. It is wholly unfair to send the people away, some having been fed and others still hungry.

3. Making God Real

Here is a difficult responsibility. Again it is a test of one's sincerity, devotion, and ability as a leader. In one service the leader hides himself and magnifies God. In another service God seems to be hidden and the attention of those who would worship is drawn to the leader.

Often the cause for this condition cannot be attributed to

any one specific thing, for usually an accumulation of conditions may be responsible. It does emphasize the seriousness of the leader's responsibility in making God real to these who assemble to worship.

It may be that the sermon offers the best opportunity to make God real. How effectively this matter can be handled is another question. Certainly the Word of God must be central, and the preaching must be Christ-centered. Men come to know God in Christ. Let the preacher draw man and God together.

But the sermon must do many things. It must deal with man and man as well as man and God. It needs to instruct in morals, in stewardship, in human relations, in missions, and so on. The sermon alone cannot make God real to the man in the pew.

But music! Here is the opportunity to do in every service what a sermon can do only occasionally. It is not only what one hears that reveals God, but what one experiences through participation. Let the people sing! In the open country church, in the villages and towns, in the city church—let all the people sing! How often leaders are tempted to sacrifice the congregational singing to make time for detailed announcements, lengthy "specials," the greeting of visitors! "We shall now sing the first and last stanzas . . . ."

People need to sing to God. They need Jesus to come to them in the hymns and gospel songs. As important as anthems are and as beautiful as the music may be, there can be in them three hindrances to worship: inadequate words, words not clearly given, and the fact that some people are not always moved by this type of music.

God becomes real to some in the Scripture reading and prayer portion of the service. Others find him more readily in the music. There are those also who experience the fuller revelation of God through the preaching of his Word. No doubt most of us find him in the total service which offers all these helps in proper balance.

4. *Maintaining Interest*

We do not know exactly how people responded in other centuries. No doubt they were far less time conscious and far less critical of the leadership. Our entertainment-trained people of today are hypercritical as well as time conscious. Accustomed as they are to watching and listening, it is hard for them to remain interested very long at a time. Minds wander. Imaginations work overtime. Some folk sleep! A well-integrated, thoroughly planned and prepared service must be properly directed if the modern congregation is to be kept alert and interested.

Successful is the pastor who has the happy faculty for welding the components of a worship service into a God-honoring whole. Such a faculty is an art, but it is one that can be acquired and cultivated. In a later chapter we shall study the steps necessary in maintaining interest. Now it is sufficient to say that one cannot make the most of an hour of worship unless he is able to blend it into one happy, soul-satisfying, victorious experience.

IV. THE PSYCHOLOGY OF ATTENTION

Having dealt with the subject of maintaining interest, we may go a step further and expand it into the theme of the psychology of attention. In the worship services today, more than ever before, attempts are being made to challenge the attention and maintain the interest. We have pointed out that few people now attend church simply because doing so is right. The service must be rewarding. To be rewarding it must of necessity be interesting enough to hold the attention and bring about a decision of some sort. The prime question comes at the close of the service, "What are you going to do as a result of this service?"

1. *Give Attention to the Setting*

In the music and education work of many churches today the "interest center" is often given a place of prominence. It is common to find large cabinets of visual aid equipment—colored table covers, spotlights, pictures—items needed to tell a story visually.

The setting is no less important in worship services. Baptists have been a little slower than some other groups to take full advantage of this fact. The more formal churches have used their tables, crosses, candles, flowers, pictures, stained windows, and other facilities throughout the years. Baptists have been careful to select only those things which give proper emphasis without offending. In Baptist churches the pulpit and the Bible are in the central position with the baptistry behind the choir and the table in front of the pulpit. Often a large Bible is set on the table; flowers are attractively placed; choirs are beautifully robed; and the various articles of furniture are properly spaced.

But the setting is not only a matter of architecture and order and arrangement of the physical properties. There is a musical setting, also. It is determined by the prelude. People should be trained to know that when the prelude begins the service begins. Why not let the pastor make his entrance exactly at that moment? Would it not help to remind the folk that talking, or even whispering, is out of place? Let the total setting gain the attention of the worshipers.

2. *The Importance of Variety*

Beware of sameness! Can you visualize the order of service in your church with your eyes closed? Is the "Doxology" always sung immediately after the prelude? Does the anthem always precede the sermon? Does the choir always sing the same responses? Variety attracts attention. It holds interest. Every part of the service needs variety.

Even the lengthiest symphonies do not become boring to the person who loves classical music because of the variety expressed in the various movements and the variations upon the main theme. So the Christian is not bored, but elated, when the "movements and themes" in the worship service lift him out of the humdrum of life.

3. *The Time Element*

"The preacher preached an hour and a half." Do you hear that remark today? Rarely. But it was commonplace years ago. Most sermons today are about thirty minutes in length. A point was made earlier concerning proper balance. Now balance is a matter of both time and content. For example, people do not resent a long anthem if it is a very good one well sung. Nor do they complain of the lengthy sermon if it is a very good one well presented.

Today, more than ever before, there is an awareness of the time problem. No doubt the fact that programs on the air are so carefully divided into half hours and hours has wielded its influence. Man has developed an inner timing device that keeps him time conscious. When we have lost the attention of the congregation we have lost the opportunity to bring man to God in a worship experience.

Blessed are those who count time as precious and give careful consideration to the psychology of attention.

4. *In Touch with the Familiar*

In worship more than in any other thing one must guard against the twin dangers of the rut of the familiar and the broad plain of the new and unfamiliar. If one were to plan a service with a completely new format—all unfamiliar hymns, a brand-new anthem, organ solos that had never been heard before—there would be little worship and a great deal of dissatisfaction.

On the other hand, a service made up of the most familiar

hymns, an often-used anthem, and a trite sermon, the effect, though not as shocking, would be about as disappointing. There must be freshness! A prelude played with an air of expectancy, a hymn with familiar tune but new words, a sermon as ancient as the Bible in text and context, but as fresh in approach as a new day. Such is the need and, we believe, the trend. Always there must be the touch with the familiar.

5. *The Sure Step*

Finally, there is in worship today an emphasis on exactness. It has already been expressed in various sections of this study, but let it be re-emphasized: The leader must know where he is going, what he needs to accomplish, and how he will accomplish it. He must walk with sure step. And the sure step in worship leadership on the part of the pastor and the minister of music is the step of adequate preparation.

FOR FURTHER STUDY AND DISCUSSION

1. Your church is either open country, village, or city; it is either small, medium, or large. In the light of this chapter, make a careful study of the music program of your church. How would you evaluate it: good, average, poor?
2. Ask your pastor, minister of music, and minister of education to let you have some bulletins which are received from other churches. Make a study of the hymns they sing, the music they use, and the order of service planned.
3. Make a careful check of all musical instruments in your church buildings. Are they adequate? Are they in tune? Discuss your findings with those who have the responsibility in your church.
4. Pay particular attention to the worship services in your own church and, from what you have learned, evaluate them as to warmth, balance, interest, and results. Do they demonstrate the reality of God?

CHAPTER 5 OUTLINE

5

Worship and the Person
in the Pew

EVERY WORSHIP SERVICE should be planned in such a way as to meet the spiritual needs of the greatest number of people. Although there is a possibility that a service might be "over-planned," a far greater injustice to those who would worship results when there is *no* planning.

Each worship service should be conducted in orderly fashion. Some churches have printed orders of service, while thousands do not. *With* or *without* a printed order, the leaders of worship should have well formulated plans in mind, preferably written out so that there will be no interruption or misunderstanding. The people will follow their leaders; the important thing is that the leaders make adequate plans. This is as essential to the open country church as it is to the large city church. Planning is necessary whether the service is an unpretentious order of service or one that is elaborate and varied. The primary objective should be to meet the spiritual needs of the man in the pew through each part of the service.

I. MEETING MAN'S SPIRITUAL NEEDS

Man is a spiritual being, created in the image of God. Despite his fall, he has an inner hunger that can only be satisfied with spiritual food. Worship is God's answer to this deep longing within the soul of man. In worship one meets God. In worship one is inspired to be more like the Master. It is evident then that the public worship service must be planned especially for the person in the pew. Never must it be taken lightly. All of the world is holding out the things that appeal to the physical man. Few offer him spiritual help. This is our task.

1. *The Understanding Leader*

In private worship the individual is his own leader. He simply reads his Bible, prays, and meditates.

Family worship provides a simple service for two or more persons where one is the leader. When there are but two, quite often they take turns leading. The head of the family has a wonderful opportunity to knit human hearts with the heart of God through the daily service at the table, in the living room, or in the room where sleep will soon overtake each one.

But we are most concerned with public worhip in church services. Proficiency of leadership is essential. Here the prophet is also priest! Being a prophet (one who speaks for God) is very important. The sermon is the main course in the spiritual meal served to the congregations. However, let no one minimize the priestly function. The trained, capable, consecrated leader is greatly needed in each church for services of worship.

Such a leader must know how to conduct public worship. His goal is to bring the people into right relationship with God and with one another. He is to make God real. He is to make the worship service interesting and distinctly Christian.

The proficient leader is perfectly at ease as he leads in prayer, reads the Scriptures, preaches the Word, and correlates the various parts of the service. Such proficiency cannot be achieved without thorough planning and preparation.

2. *Worship or Entertainment?*

We have said that the service is to be made interesting. True. Attention must be held! But how carefully the distinction must be made between that which is conducive to worship and that which is merely entertaining! The worship leader needs to guard against being a master of ceremonies. The minister of music, while striving for perfection in every phase of the music program, must see that it is not a performance for the purpose of entertaining. Such leadership is perhaps the most difficult to achieve. Truly, worship leadership is an art. And no one works harder or is more dedicated than a real artist.

It is wise here to insist that every excess be avoided. Let no jarring note be sounded. The man in the pew has come to meet God. He who sends the people away without vision or hope has missed the central point of his ministry.

There are four main sections of an order of service, whether printed in the bulletin or not. These are: Worship in Praise, Worship in Prayer, Worship in Giving, and Worship in Dedication of Life. Each of these has a place for music. In fact, the musical entries outnumber all others combined.

II. WORSHIP IN PRAISE

Now we begin a detailed study of the order of service for worship. If we include everything that is used by all the churches, we shall have a full program.

1. *The Power of the Prelude*

One of the definitions of the word *prelude* is "that which foreshadows a coming event." This meaning fits our concept of the organ or piano prelude. It sets the tempo for the whole service. Opera lovers will call to mind the preludes to their favorite operas. In them are sweet reminders of great love, the thunderings of impending doom, and the throb of coming heartbreak. Then, as the story unfolds, bits of music reach back into the prelude and seem to say, "I told you so."

In like manner the prelude to a worship service should foreshadow that which is to come.

How unfortunate that many congregations obliterate the prelude with chatter! What can one expect of an organist who realizes that his every effort is wasted?

The person in the pew who truly wants to worship God lets the music of the prelude set the spiritual tempo of his soul. He walks in the Garden of Eden. He stands at the foot of Jacob's ladder. He lives with Isaiah his mighty vision. He visits Bethlehem or Capernaum or Nazareth. He stands by the tomb of Lazarus. He is in the upper room with Jesus. He stands under the old olive tree in Gethsemane. With Peter he warms himself by the fire. He walks the *via dolorosa*, stands at the foot of the cross, at the open tomb, on the mount of ascension. He worships!

How can one prefer visiting with his fellow members to the spiritual fellowship he may enjoy? Is it right to lift one's voice higher and higher to overcome the organ's message? Let the prelude exert its influence. It has power. Let it speak.

2. *The Call to Worship*

Some churches use a processional hymn. Others use an opening selection sung by the choir. Still others employ the verbal call to worship consisting of a Bible verse or a well-stated invitation to worship.

If a choir is to use a processional hymn, it will be necessary to institute processional procedures. For instance, it must be determined whether the processional should be a marching or a walking processional. Authorities seem to be in somewhat general agreement that the unmarched processional possesses greater beauty, since it is less aggressive, smoother, and less likely to have secular associations. "Lead On, O King of Eternal," "Soldiers of Christ, Arise," "The Son of God Goes Forth to War," "Who Is on the Lord's Side?" "Stand Up, Stand Up for Jesus," "Once to Every Man and Nation," "My Soul, Be on Thy Guard," and "Arise, O Youth of God," are just a few of the hymns appropriate for a processional.

The use of the processional hymn does not rule out the verbal call to worship. Those not desiring the processional or wishing to vary the order of service will have the choir sing the call to worship. Some suggested hymns for this are: "God, Our Father, We Adore Thee," "Praise to the Lord, the Almighty," "Let All on Earth Their Voices Raise," "Praise the Lord! Ye Heavens, Adore Him," "Stand Up, and Bless the Lord," "Now to the Lord a Noble Song," and "The Spacious Firmament." Some portions of anthems also lend themselves readily to this part of the service.

The Scripture selection is invaluable as a call to worship. See how effective it is when the worship leader steps to the pulpit and speaks clearly and accurately: "Prepare ye the way of the Lord, make straight in the desert a highway for our God. And the glory of the Lord shall be revealed, and all flesh shall see it together: for the mouth of the Lord hath spoken it. . . . Blessed be the King that cometh in the name of the Lord: peace in heaven, and glory in the highest" (Isa. 40:3, 5; Luke 19:38).

"Arise, shine; for thy light is come, and the glory of the Lord is risen upon thee. . . . Lift up thine eyes round about, and see: . . . ." (Isa. 60:1, 4).

"Sing and rejoice, . . . for, lo, I come, and I will dwell in the midst of thee, saith the Lord. . . . It is high time to awake out of sleep: for now is our salvation nearer than when we believed. The night is far spent, the day is at hand: let us therefore cast off the works of darkness, and let us put on the armour of light" (Zech. 2:10; Rom. 13:11–12).

"In this was manifested the love of God toward us, because that God sent his only begotten Son into the world, that we might live through him. . . . For God, who commanded the light to shine out of darkness, hath shined in our hearts, to give the light of the knowledge of the glory of God in the face of Jesus Christ" (1 John 4:9; 2 Cor. 4:6).

"O send out thy light and thy truth: let them lead me; let them bring me unto thy holy hill, and to thy tabernacles. Then will I go unto the altar of God, unto God my exceeding joy" (Psalm 43:3-4).

"Behold, I stand at the door, and knock: if any man hear my voice, and open the door, I will come in to him, and will sup with him, and he with me" (Rev. 3:20).

"God also hath highly exalted him, and given him a name which is above every name: that at the name of Jesus every knee should bow, of things in heaven, and things in earth, and things under the earth; and that every tongue should confess that Jesus Christ is Lord, to the glory of God the Father" (Phil. 2:9-11).

"The Spirit and the bride say, Come. . . . And let him that is athirst come. And whosoever will, let him take the water of life freely" (Rev. 22:17).

"Lord, thou has been our dwelling place in all generations. Before the mountains were brought forth, or ever thou hadst formed the earth and the world, even from everlasting to everlasting, thou art God" (Psalm 90:1-2).

The use of the "Doxology" is appropriate at this point or even following the invocation.

3. The Invocation

The call to worship should have the attention of the man in the pew. Now he is ready for prayer. It is a brief prayer invoking God's blessing upon the people in the service of worship. This is not the time for a long prayer. Brevity is essential. Every word needs to be exactly right. Let us cite a few examples:

> Our Father, we give thee our thanks for the re-creation of body and mind thou hast given us in the hours of wonderful

sleep. But now help us to be awake and alert as we face a new day. It is thy day. Help us to honor thee in it.

We come, gracious Lord, in the spirit of worship with songs of praise on our lips. Accept our worship; strengthen our purpose; and increase our usefulness.

We pray in Jesus' name. Amen.

Thy Word, O Lord, is a lamp unto our feet and a light unto our path. We pray that we may be good stewards of that Word, carrying as true ambassadors the light of the gospel to a waiting world.

Lead us, we pray, into a service of worship that will bring glory to thy name and cleansing to our souls. Amen.

Our loving Father in heaven, the darkness of this morning hour of lowering clouds reminds us of the darkness of Calvary when sin seemed to triumph over grace. Let thy light shine through these clouds even as thy victory was won over the powers of sin and darkness on that dread day.

We yield unto thee our hearts for cleansing, our bodies as instruments for divine service. Make them wholly thine we pray in Jesus' name. Amen.

Dear Lord, as the old year ends and the new year begins, forgive us for the failures of the vanished days, and bless us in whatever we have truly tried to accomplish for thy kingdom. Keep us from vain regrets, and let us face forward in the light of the best that we have learned from thee. Purge our hearts from shallow self-confidence and cowardly fears, and make of us a blessing to others.

In Jesus' blessed name we pray. Amen.

Occasionally, a pastor may wish to write out his prayer. If so, the invocation would be the logical one to write. Later, will come the free outpouring of the heart in the shepherd's prayer for his flock. The invocation may easily "make or break" the spirit of worship.

This is not the time to call on someone in the congregation to pray! Discussion of this matter will come later.

In some churches the invocation is followed by the "Gloria Patri" or some other response sung by the choir or by choir and congregation. Such a procedure can be exceedingly effective. Thousands of churches, however, are not yet ready for such formalities. The wise leader will use variety, studying carefully the response of the people. That which aids in worship is good. If it offends in any way it should be omitted. If it is good it may be attempted at a later time.

4. *Solo, Anthem, or Congregational Hymn*

The final part of the section Worship in Praise is musical. Some use a solo. Others prefer an anthem. The vast majority of worship leaders use a congregational hymn. Again there is opportunity for variety. Whichever of these three is used, let it be a song of praise!

The people need to participate as much as possible in the service. Great benefits are derived from such participation. Prayer in unison is difficult; the solo and anthem put the people in the position of being listeners. Let the people sing!

III. WORSHIP IN PRAYER

There is no part of the minister's function more important, more vital, more sacred, than public prayer. In a Christian worship service prayer largely takes the place that sacrifice held among the Hebrews. As there were several different sacrifices in Hebrew worship, there are various kinds of prayers. The chief desire of the worshiper is to be right with God and do his holy will. Not with sacrifices, but with prayers, he will seek wisdom and strength to accomplish his purpose.

The worship leader's task is to help people know that God is real, present, ready to hear and bless. Often a prayer seems to be *for* the hearer more than *to* God. Herein lies the difficulty. Public praying is difficult. The prayer is definitely to God, but it is designed to lead the worshiper in such a way as to help him feel it is his own prayer. The wise leader realizes his prayer must bring to mind man's sin and God's mercy and pardoning grace. The prayer should express desire for dedication of life to God for Jesus' sake.

The invocation, of which we wrote earlier, is the most difficult to plan because it must be brief and simple. The opening of the prayer, which addresses the Father, the Son, or the Holy Spirit, should be followed by a relative clause stating some attribute or promise. The petition should follow the expression of a simple statement of desire. There should be a valid reason for every petition to God. Let it be expressed! The key phrase is "in order that" or one similar to it. We want God to know why we desire his help. The conclusion for the Christian cannot omit the honest expression, "through Jesus Christ our Lord," "in Christ's name," or a similar expression.

In large auditoriums the practice of calling on persons in the congregation to lead in prayer is usually unwise. Why? Because such prayers are lost except to God. Is it not enough that he hear? No! Public prayer is for every mind and heart. Let the leader, if he feels it advisable to call on others to lead in prayer, plan ahead and have them with him on the rostrum.

Offertory prayers, especially when a man's back is to the congregation, are mere mumblings to the ears of the people.

How much better it is to plan the public prayer even as one plans the sermon and the song.

1. *Reading God's Word*

This second section in the order of service, Worship in Prayer, usually begins with the reading of God's Word. It may be read in unison, responsively, or by the leader. Here again variety is advisable. Keep in mind that this is a part of worship; that it is seldom wise to read the selection to be used for the sermon. The reading should prepare the way for prayer! One needs to spend a great deal of time in searching the Bible for passages that are definite aids to worship.

There is a difference of opinion concerning the wisdom

of using the responsive or unison readings. The one who insists on variety will have no problem. If the desired selection is in the hymnal, use it. If not, let the pastor read it from his Bible.

Whether one uses one method or all three, the matter is still one of proper leadership. The minister should be schooled in correct reading. Attention should be given to tempo and expression. A monotonous droning gives no clear message from God. In order to execute this important part effectively it is necessary to practice. If the singer needs to rehearse, so does the reader.

People need to be trained in the fine art of public worship. The new minister should first study the pattern familiar to the people and then lead them, without their being conscious of it, into a richer, fuller worship experience.

We are "people of the Book." Let us make the most of it.

2. *Meditation*

The stilted, "So endeth the reading of the lesson," still used by some leaders, raises something of a barrier against the important pastoral prayer. It is so easy to blend the Bible reading into the prayer with a brief organ meditation. There is time to think of the words just read; time to make them personal. The music, if wisely chosen and thoughtfully played, will do no more than reach a hand to the Word and another to the prayer and draw them together. What more is desired?

3. *The Pastoral Prayer*

The pastoral prayer, while longer than the invocation, should not exceed three to five minutes. It must be kept in mind that the pastor is not only praying for his flock; he is leading them to walk with the Shepherd. They must not wander or be lost along the way. A helpful pattern for the leader to follow is: thanksgiving, petition, supplication, commitment. The lost, the sick, the needy, the puzzled, the distressed should all be remembered. Leave not one person untouched.

4. *Choral Response*

Many churches use a choral response after the Shepherd's prayer. It is a fitting thing to do. Most common is "Hear Our Prayer, O Lord," but there are several others that can well be used to avoid the rut of changeless procedure. How music undergirds the whole service of worship!

IV. WORSHIP IN GIVING

Stewardship is so very important that it is wise to plan a complete section in the worship service on worship in giving. Some part of this section may need to be used to instruct the people or to make a special plea. Such is never out of place if it is thoughtfully and skilfully done.

1. *A Hymn of Dedication*

Before the men, whether deacons or ushers, come down the aisle, there is usually a hymn sung by the congregation. How many stanzas should be sung? Wisdom will dictate. The hymn itself must be taken into consideration—its length in measures, the number of stanzas, and the message expressed in the song. Some hymns demand the use of every stanza to complete their message. Others can be effective with only one stanza used. If possible, the decision should be made in the planning stage and printed in the bulletin. Otherwise, there may be confusion, or pressure for time may cause a crippling of the message.

A prayer usually precedes or follows the taking of the offering. As much care needs to be exercised in this as in the other prayers. Some use the "Doxology" as an offertory prayer.

2. *The Offertory*

Music reigns again. The organist or pianist is obligated to prepare the most fitting music for the moment. The purpose is clear. There is not only a brief span of time to fill to keep the continuity of the service, but music has an effect on the giving spirit of the man in the pew. No dirge. No jig. Let there be joy, life, sparkle. There is joy in giving. We should feel it in the music.

Brevity is a necessity. No matter how great the organ or how skilled the organist, when the offering has been taken there is a restlessness until the choir rises or the soloist utters the first note. Have you heard an organist say, "I will no more cut my offertory than the preacher will cut his sermon"? But the preacher does cut his sermon! Often too drastically, only because the offertory and the anthem have used too much time. Many services are broadcast or televised. At twelve o'clock the end will come, ready or not. The studious organist can easily plan several ways of achieving an ending without "butchering" the piece.

V. WORSHIP IN THE DEDICATION OF LIFE

The final section in the order of service brings the worship hour to a climax. The ground has been prepared. Human hearts have touched God. Now it is time for great inspiration, instruction, convincing argument, and exhortation.

1. *The Anthem or Solo*

If ever the preacher and the musicians need to be of one mind and one heart it is now. There must be no cleavage. This does not mean that the anthem and the sermon can always fit hand in glove. But surely the two will complement each other. Without appearing to be giving a performance, the musicians will present a message or touch an emotion that will open the doors of the hearts and minds for the preaching of the gospel.

2. *The Sermon*

Man's needs are many; his spiritual hungers run deep and wide. The physical man is not satisfied with one or two items of food—the same yesterday, today, and forever. So it is with the spirit and mind of man.

The sermon should reflect diligent study, earnest prayer, personal concern, and attention to every detail. It should be clearly spoken, interestingly presented, and definitely personal. It should be brief enough to hold the interest and long enough to present a sound case and press for decision. We preach for results. Not merely public commitments, but results that are praiseworthy in daily living.

3. *Hymn of Invitation*

Not all churches of other denominations use an invitation. The universal practice, however, is to employ a closing hymn. Southern Baptist churches almost invariably sing a true hymn of invitation while the pastor "draws the net."

Of all the items in the order of service none offers a greater "chance" of failure than this one. It must be kept in mind, however, that the failure to have additions to the church is not always a mark of defeat. Personal response may be made in the heart without being made in public.

The real failure is found when the people simply go away. The service is over; minds quickly shift to other things; there is no action because there was actually no decision.

But it cannot be denied that the invitation hymn can also mean the difference between victory and defeat. Never is it to be a new one! Invitation hymns need to be sung easily, almost from memory. New ones may be sung by the choir until they become familiar to the congregation.

Tempo is of genuine importance, too. If the pace is too fast, the effect will probably be destroyed. If there is a mournful dragging, the invitation dies a slow death. The correct hymn, properly sung, with a warm, carefully stated invitation is apt to reach the person in the pew with an appeal that cannot be ignored.

4. *Benediction and Response*

Most of the churches use a choir response after the benediction. In it there is a spiritual penetration, a last thrust that is needed. Moreover, it gives the minister an opportunity to place himself at a door before the exodus begins so that he can give a warm and cordial greeting to the members, especially to the visitors.

5. *The Postlude*

People seldom hear the postlude. They are aware that the organ is being played, but they are engaged in conversation, or they are greeting the new members. Such a situation is not bad! The people are not expected to stand quietly awaiting the organ's last note; nor are they to file out as if leaving a funeral service. The postlude can have a good effect if used properly. What is proper?

Bombastic music sends folk away often in disgust or anger. They have tried to be cordial to friends and newcomers. Their efforts have been drowned out by the thundering tones of the organ. The music should be warm, friendly, cordial, conducive to harmony among all the people.

VI. SOME VARIATIONS

Have you ever honestly analyzed your Sunday evening worship services? Does each person have an individual, practical, and vital worship experience? Three key words need consideration in planning worship services that afford such benefits: motive, balance, and variety.

1. *The Evening Hour of Worship*

Briefly, the Sunday evening hour of worship majors on congregational singing and vigorous preaching. Rarely are responses or responsive readings used. Freedom within carefully defined limits is advisable.

People will still attend church at night if they know that they will receive a blessing. If we put more into the evening service, there will be more people receiving more from it!

2. *Beware of the Rut*

Someone has said that a rut is a grave with the ends knocked out. The advice has been given again and again in these discussions: Use variety! The easy way is to employ the same format month after month, year after year. But the easy way is the way of the rut. The secret of a great ministry is eternal freshness under the direction of the Holy Spirit.

FOR FURTHER STUDY AND DISCUSSION

1. For your own practical study, plan several orders of service for both morning and evening worship. Be especially conscious of balance, which is achieved by giving ample time and place for praise, prayer, giving, and dedication of life.
2. Make it a point to have a brief personal conference with each of the leaders in church music and worship. Plan pertinent questions in advance.
3. As you study MUSIC IN WORSHIP, put your thoughts on paper. Reread the book or certain parts of it, and then rethink your paper on the subject.

CHAPTER 6 OUTLINE

Leadership of Public Worship

It is imperative that Christians, assembled in public worship, should be spiritually enriched. It is necessary therefore for those who lead in worship to sense the deepest needs of those they seek to lead.

The leader must realize the woeful folly of inadequate, ineffective, and careless planning and preparation. On the other hand, his greatest sense of satisfaction will come from seeing men drawn closer to God through a sincere, personal experience of worship. Only when the leader is fully acquainted with his responsibilities, and possesses the know-how and the will for fulfilling them will these experiences be possible.

I. The Place of the Pastor

Impressive and spiritually uplifting worship services reflect the vision and leadership ability of the pastor. Just as he is pastor of the Sunday school, Training Union, Music Ministry, and other church organizations, he is the leader of worship for his members and others who worship in his church.

By this we do not mean that he must actively lead or direct each part of the service, but rather that he should take an active interest in each progressive step of the service. He is the co-ordinator. He will enlist others according to their specific abilities and leadership qualities.

1. *Leadership in Worship*

In almost every case the pastor of the church is the worship leader. There are a few churches whose pastor remains seated while another—usually the music director—conducts the service. If the music director is better trained and more adept at leading worship, it is better for the preacher to sit and wait.

It is the privilege of the leader to utilize others in the service. He can do so effectively if he plans well in advance. It is destructive, however, to call on people on the spur of the moment to pray, to make announcements, to give testimony. Such cannot be called leadership.

The requirements for leadership are high. A warm heart and a firm hand, made ready by prayer and planning, are vitally necessary to a successful hour of worship. Who should be better fitted for this than the pastor of the church?

2. Thorough Knowledge and Training

Ignorance here is inexcusable. Greater ease and facility in leadership will come with experience, but there is no excuse for lack of knowledge. Book stores are well stocked with volumes designed to help the individual train himself in the fine art of worship leadership. Those who work in the stores are usually qualified to suggest the most helpful sources.

It is wise for the pastor to be alert to study the new books that arrive at the stores. Men are constantly laboring in the field of worship, even as scientists are endeavoring to uncover truths in chemistry, physics, and the like. The field is a broad one, demanding constant interest.

One of the sad errors of so many pastors is that of neglecting the subject of church music. One says, "I am simply not musical." Such is not a good excuse. He probably is not a linguist, but he may have learned the rudiments of Greek, Hebrew, and Latin. He is no historian, but he learned church history. It is not necessary that he be an instrumentalist or a vocal soloist. But to be totally uninformed concerning church music is inexcusable.

Thorough knowledge of this field will not only make the pastor a good leader of worship services—it will make him an understanding team leader when working with the choir director, organist, pianist, and music council.

3. *The Growing Preacher*

The preacher in most of our churches is an administrator, counselor, pastor, builder, and tactician, as well as a preacher of the gospel. With the training he has received he is equipped to accept the responsibility of a pastorate. But he is a beginner. Like a physician recently graduated from medical school, he has the tools and some skill, but lacks experience. The success of the preacher, like that of the doctor, depends on his growth. Growth is the product of constant study and practice. In the field of medicine there are new products and new techniques streaming from the schools and laboratories. The minister of the gospel faces the task of keeping up with the ever-expanding field of the ministry. Books and magazines, conferences and clinics offer constant help.

Worship is as essential to the soul as is physical nourishment to the body. The Lord wants both body and soul saved for his use and his glory. Yes, a preacher needs to grow!

II. The Minister of Music

The term "minister of music" is often used interchangeably with "director of music." The minister of music usually gives his full time to the church; the director of music serves as a part-time worker, either with or without remuneration. Far more churches have leaders serving part time than full time. This does not minimize the need for the highest spiritual and professional standards for the leader.

1. *A Difficult Vocation*

The place of the minister of music in the churches is not new in this generation, but it has been greatly expanded. Never before has the task been so great.

No matter how excellent his musicianship, the minister of music has the problem of satisfying the music preferences of the congregation, the pastor, the choirs, the soloists, and the instrumentalists. In his heart he knows what the Lord wants accomplished in a worship service and in a church music program. Others may not agree with him. Varying opinions are almost inevitable. What grace is required! What gentleness of spirit! The place is an important one and difficult to fill.

2. *Background and Training*

An individual's background has much to do with his ability to cope with the various situations in a church. Fortunate is he who has spent his life in church activities. Even more fortunate is he who has experienced life in churches in the country, town, and city, gaining thereby an understanding of the variety of needs and problems.

Greatly blessed is the individual who has a music background. When good music is a part of the life at home and at school, the young person has a distinct advantage when launching on a music career.

However, lack of music background does not rule out the probability of success in the church music field. There may even be some advantage in not having to undo or "unlearn" some of the things that often attend the music experiences of youth.

Talent and training are more important than background, helpful as it is. These two, talent and training, go together. They are inseparable. The greatest talent is almost useless unless it is trained. The best training possible accomplishes little without talent. It is also true that there is often a real talent that is latent until adequate training opens the door.

3. *Qualifications*

No one person can meet all the desired qualifications. It is dangerous, however, to employ one who cannot meet the majority of them. And some are absolutely essential to effective leadership.

The music director should be a person of Christian character. His influence is great, and he should be a constant source of inspiration to those with whom he deals. If a church must choose between two individuals, one an outstanding musician but weak in Christian character and the other a true Christian but less talented in music, it will do well to choose the latter.

Moreover, the minister of music in a church should be a loyal church member, having a radiant personality, neat appearance, pleasing voice, co-operative spirit, sense of humor, true humility, and thorough music knowledge. He needs to know Sunday school and Training Union organization, curriculum, and procedure. His knowledge of the Bible should be far above average.

4. A Tactful Leader

Tact is one of the most important requirements for the minister of music. He is a team member, having his share of responsibility for the church. He works with both paid and volunteer workers, dealing constantly with persons of various ages and backgrounds.

Saying the right thing is just as important as doing the right thing. What one says and the tone of his voice will not only determine the effectiveness of one's ministry, but will often determine how long one is to hold his place of leadership. One of the most tactless approaches is that of prodding or criticizing others publicly. If correction is necessary, let the director speak to the one in private. There is little chance of offense if the group is corrected; but beware of singling out individuals.

Many good musicians have ruined their effectiveness by giving way to temper or by speaking sharply to persons in the music family of the church.

5. *Too Many "Irons in the Fire"*

The minister of music is expected to give his full measure of devotion to his task. He must be neither a clock puncher nor one who plays at the job. Music is full-time work. If one is a "combination man" he simply has two full-time jobs. It is almost impossible to give maximum service in both music and education. The work in one area will alternately suffer while that of the other will flourish, or both may suffer.

The leader who has charge of the music program of the church needs to beware of having too many "irons in the fire." Few leaders have sufficient help to attempt all the desired activities of a fully-graded music program. The part of wisdom is to develop the program gradually, starting with that which is absolutely indispensable, and working out the expansion as time and facilities permit. Many directors have started so ambitiously that the resultant failure was interpreted as lack of ability or laziness. It is far better to do a few things well than to spread a thin program over a large area.

In music, as in every other field, it is easy to accept too many obligations in the community. Denominational work cannot be evaded and should not be neglected. But, the church must have first place. And within the church program, the worship services must have the best leadership one has to offer.

6. *Team Member*

No matter how small the church staff may be, the minister of music is a member of the team. When a church is strong enough to employ a minister of music, it is certain that there will be a pastor, a secretary, an organist (or pianist), and a custodian. Almost without exception there will be a minister of education also. The largest churches usually employ a staff of several persons with special training for their duties.

This fact puts the minister of music in a position where patience and generosity of spirit are absolute necessities. The pastor is the team captain. He may or may not be easy to work with. The church work will stand or fall upon the rock or sand of staff relationships. By all means, it must be a spiritual relationship which rules out pettiness, jealousy, suspicion, and bigotry.

III. FULL-TIME JOB

Whether the person responsible for the church music is a part-time or full-time worker, he has a full-time job. This is just as true of the small church as the large one, the open-country church or the village or city church. The job can be as big and as important as one makes it.

1. *Vision*

The problem in the churches for many years was one of vision; vision on the part of the people; vision on the part of the pastor. Most often the music leader was severely handicapped because of the lack of vision in others.

However, the director himself may be at fault. Vision is restricted by ignorance, expanded by knowledge. A man whose training has been inadequate and whose background in church life has been meager will usually be shortsighted. Proper guidance by the pastor and regular attendance at conferences and schools will help to correct poor vision. Reading bulletins from other churches will do much to enlarge one's horizon.

It is hoped that increased vision will also reveal one's shortcomings and drive him on to higher and nobler desires for self-improvement.

2. *As a Song Leader*

Leadership in singing is vitally necessary in all our churches. One person having a special talent in this field may be at his best leading the congregational singing. Another, specially fitted for choral leadership, may dread the responsibility of leading the people in the congregation. Each needs to study his own points of strength and weakness and work hard to improve where improvement is most needed. The minister of music should be able to lead singing. He should also be able to train others to lead for various departments and groups meeting in the church.

A song leader should have a sincere love both for the Lord and the people. A warm friendly attitude needs to be in evidence always. There is a place for gentle prodding, but none for scolding.

The successful song leader has a good sense of rhythm, maintains correct tempo, and puts the proper accents into the singing. He can adapt himself and his work to changing needs and unforeseen situations. All the people need to sing. But some cannot or will not attempt many of the songs. The wise leader will plan carefully so as to leave no one out.

He will compliment the people. Encourage them. Draw them with love! There is no place for cheap tricks and wisecracks. With a warm, friendly smile and a good sense of rhythm even a poor voice can be outweighed. Let all the people sing!

3. *As a Choir Director*

In addition to the leadership of congregational singing the minister of music also has the choir responsibility. He is a choir director as well as a song leader. The tasks are far different. One cannot successfully deal with a congregation on the choir level, or with the choir on a congregational level. Each has its own place.

The work with the choir demands more strictness and attention to details. One strives for perfection in sounds and effects. Many hours of work must be given to this task—hours of planning, part rehearsals, individual rehearsals for soloists and for persons who do not read music well, rehearsals for the whole choir, and the actual worship services. In addition to having the ability and training to lead choirs, the minister of music must be able to train others to lead various youth and children's choirs.

4. *As a Teacher*

It is the business of the minister of music to teach music. If he cannot teach, he has missed his calling. Indeed, there may be persons in his choir who have had superior formal training in theory, in voice, or in playing instruments. But they will be sympathetic and most helpful if he has the right attitude. Often the organist has a more thorough knowledge of music fundamentals than has the director. However, he can, if he will, continue to learn as well as to enlist those with excellent training in helping in the total program. Separate rehearsals of the four parts will afford further opportunity to use talented members as sectional leaders.

The director is a teacher! He is a teacher of music theory. The adults may be afraid of such a new thing at first, but the children love it. Indeed, some of the same musical games used with the younger choirs may be used successfully with young people and adults.

The music program of a church is indeed a full-time job for any man or woman. Many churches now have ten or twelve choirs. Some of these are so large that they have to be divided into sections. There are worship services, prayer meetings, revival meetings, music for departments, associational meetings, and many others—all demanding the talents and abilities, time and energies of the music director.

IV. INSTRUMENTALISTS

The vast majority of the churches use instruments in the worship services as well as in other church meetings. There is a growing demand for well-trained organists and pianists.

1. *Qualifications*

The spiritual qualifications should be as high for the instrumentalists as for the music director! The training should include not only music skills but an understanding of church worship services. Conservatory training does not necessarily make one a good church musician. There is a special art in playing hymns and gospel songs.

By all means, a church organist should learn to transpose music, if not at sight, then with pen and paper. Many good voices have failed to give their best because a song was written a little too high or too low for comfortable singing. Even the congregation will appreciate a slight transposition of some of the hymns.

2. *The Role of the Accompanist*

The accompanist is a team member, too. In some instances the organist is also the director. In most cases the organist or pianist is responsible directly to the minister of music. The relationship should be one of mutual confidence and complete compatability.

No other musician has more opportunities for solo work than has the church organist. We cannot emphasize too strongly the fact that the instrumentalists are members of a team with equal rights and privileges. Equal and no more.

3. *The Soloist*

The instrumental soloist may be the pianist, organist, violinist, cellist, marimbaphonist, or, occasionally, trombonist. Like the vocal soloist, he can be very good or very bad. The wise director will be quite firm in seeing that no solo detracts from the service or offends the congregation.

Please do not misunderstand. A truly beautiful and worshipful instrumental solo has great value and should be encouraged. As has been pointed out, the organist or pianist is called upon for the major solo work. Let the music fit the service. The same kind of careful planning needs to go into the instrumental work that goes into the rest of the service.

4. *Accompanist*

The accompanist should be exactly what the word implies. Not a director, not a leader, not a soloist, but an accompanist. The director, right or wrong, sets the tempo. The soloist, good or poor, is to be followed. The music, unless rehearsed differently, should be played as written. Many singers have had a difficult time because they were thrown off key by an inaccurately played accompaniment. It is exceedingly important that accompaniments be exact—accompaniments for hymns and anthems as well as solos.

Some organists are taught to play the entire hymn before the congregation begins to sing. Such is usually considered bad taste. The director should plan with the organist exactly what introductions to use. A good practice is to use the opening phrase or the closing phrase, always ending on the tonic chord. Now and then an accompanist plays an introduction, leaving it "up in the air" where neither soloist nor congregation can find the right note. Such usually happens with an instrumentalist who cannot sing. Happy is the director of music who works with an accompanist who knows vocal as well as instrumental music.

V. TEAMWORK

Time after time we have mentioned the team. And we haven't yet finished talking about it. The team cannot be over-emphasized. Co-operation is the secret of success. The best example one can use is the symphony orchestra. From sixty to one hundred musicians strive to make majestic music for the listening audience. On the podium is the conductor—the team captain. He is absolute master; yet he is a team member. There are other leaders. The concertmaster is on the team. So are the several principals of sections. There are several flutists, but there is definitely a *first* flutist. The man with the upright tuba on his knees may not play a hundred measures all evening; the harpist may sit with folded hands most of the time; but they are on the team. Their parts are essential.

1. *The Team Captain*

On a church staff the pastor is the captain of the team. At his best he is a guide, counselor, and friend. At his worst he is a dictator. As captain it is his responsibility to know the entire church program and direct it. But he cannot be expected to know more of education than does the minister of education, more music than does the minister of music, more of child psychology than does the elementary director. On his team he has specialists in the various fields.

On a great basketball team there are men who are specialists. One is noted for his outside shooting, another for his ability to break in under the basket. Still another is a defensive specialist. The playmaker is the brains and the speed of the team. The fifth man works into the team where strength is needed. The victory is a team victory; the loss is a team loss. So it is with our churches. Each staff member has his place, and is honored for his ability and energy. The team captain is the playmaker. Everything stands or falls on the pastor's ability to correlate the talents of all staff members.

2. *Each Member Important*

It has been made clear already that each member of the staff is important to the work. Differences in position and salary do not minimize the importance of the place of service held by each individual. For example, in the Music Ministry the music secretary has a long tedious task every week calling, writing, contacting, making records, preparing refreshments, perhaps accompanying. The organist on the other hand plays for several services each week, attends one or more rehearsals, and practices a few hours. There is a wide gap in the salary scale. The service of one is far more in the public eye than that of the other. Yet each is indispensable to the program. Both are important.

3. *Whose Is the Glory?*

There is no possible way to keep out of the spotlight in public service. The pastor leads, prays, reads, preaches, greets people at the door. The minister of music conducts the ensembles in their musical numbers, leads the congregation in singing, and sits on the rostrum in view of everyone. The organist comes in early, plays the prelude, hymns, offertory, accompanies the anthem, plays the postlude. The choir stands and sings and sits down. The soloists move to the "mike." The spotlight is on the leaders in worship.

How natural that people should compliment them. But whose is the glory? If those who lead have the right spirit and do their work with skill and modesty, God will have the glory. Jesus commanded us to let our light shine before men that God might have the glory (Matt. 5:16).

FOR FURTHER STUDY AND DISCUSSION

1. List the following information in your notebook: where your pastor and your minister of music attended school; what conferences on music and service planning they have attended.
2. For your own information make a list of all the tasks which fall upon your pastor. This can be done both by observation and through a personal conference. Do the same thing with the work of your minister of music whether he has music alone or music and education.
3. If you are not a choir member, make it a point to attend some rehearsals as an observer. Evaluate what you see and hear in the light of your study of this text.

CHAPTER 7 OUTLINE

7

Planning the Worship Services

"PLAN YOUR WORK; WORK YOUR PLAN." This sage advice is
sound. The basic principle of this statement has determined
one extreme or another—impressive or ineffective, inspiring or
uninspiring, orderly or chaotic, challenging or depressing,
and so on. Worship services are not an exception. Each one
should be planned with painstaking finesse.

I. THE PERSONS CONCERNED

Anything worth doing is worthy of proper and adequate
planning. An unplanned activity that proceeds without form
and direction is usually ineffective and unprofitable.

Let us consider those who regularly have responsibilities
for planning worship services.

1. *The Pastor*

The major responsibility for planning the worship services,
as well as the leadership of them, rests on the pastor of the
church. Before he consults with any person on the staff or in
the church membership he must talk with the Lord. The
whole program of worship should be conceived in prayer.

A great deal of study and thought needs to go into the
minister's preparation. Aware of the needs of his own heart
and the needs of his people, he will think first of the sermon.
It may be determined by the church calendar, the evident
spiritual need of some persons or the entire membership,
recent happenings in the nation or the community. Or, it may
follow normally in the use of a series covering a subject or

one whole book of the Bible. However the sermon idea comes, it is central in the mind of the shepherd of souls.

With the sermon in mind he uses his hymnal. The minister should be as familiar with the hymnal as with the Bible. This means the hymns, gospel songs, responses, selected Bible readings—everything. It does not mean that he needs to fit every hymn to the sermon subject. It is far wiser to make the first hymn in a morning service one of worship and praise. The next one will be one of the devotional type—of dedication or consecration. In the evening service the gospel song will be used freely. Both pastor and minister of music should be well qualified to choose the hymns for a service, but they will do their best work by planning together. This meeting of the minds will be most fruitful.

The whole order soon takes shape: the call to worship, reading of the Word, special music, etc. Why should people speak of special music when Sunday after Sunday it is given the same place in the order of service? It is no more special than the sermon or the hymn of invitation.

Many pastors plan several weeks or even months in advance. For the sake of variety, the order is changed a little week after week. The difference is slight, but helpful. With such future planning, the music director will be able to do his best work. The pastor is then ready for the music staff conference, whether weekly or monthly.

2. *Minister of Music*

The minister of music also needs to plan ahead. He should know months in advance a great many anthems and solos he wants to use. Some of these will be new, some old and often used. Several of them should be held in reserve, ready for selection. In conference with the pastor, right choices will usually be made.

If the minister of music plays the piano, it is wise for him to spend much time playing hymns new and old. Not only does he need to have definite opinions concerning the rhythms and tempos, but even more important, the messages of the songs.

If he does not play the piano, he should enlist the organist or church pianist to help in making such studies. When the time comes for the important planning conference, he should have in mind and at his finger tips anthems, solos, hymns, and responses to suggest to the leader.

3. *Instrumentalists*

By all means the organist and/or pianist should be present at the conference. Their wisdom and skill are needed. Moreover, they need to be aware of every careful detail of planning. These two should be well prepared with materials, lists of preludes, offertories, and postludes. These musicians should possess a thorough knowledge of the message within each piece. Naturally, many pretty tunes that actually have no worship significance will be ruled out.

4. *By Invitation*

Certain persons should be invited into the worship planning conferences from time to time. It does not take long to learn who the sincere critics are. Many times, teams pass up good opportunities to study the worship service from the viewpoint of the participant in the congregation.

The choir president, choir librarian, minister of education, and others may well be included on occasions; not all at one time, of course. Now we should be ready for the planning conference.

II. THE PROCEDURE

When the participants convene, the pastor will be in charge of the conference.

1. *Prayer Time*

It is essential that workers pray together. No matter how the individuals have prayed in their private planning, there is need for group prayer. It may be a prayer led by the pastor or any one of the group, or it may be a chain of prayers.

2. *Evident Preparation*

We have pointed out the wisdom of individual preparation. Such preparation or the lack of it will soon be in evidence. As the leader moves from point to point, the strengths and weaknesses will be revealed. Such revelations immediately point up the value of the conference and make each individual conscious of his need to be better prepared.

3. *General Matters*

The pastor will no doubt open the discussion with a few words of appreciation and commendation. Then he will give his own appraisal of the work during the past service or services. He will review the orders of service as given in the bulletin and will ask for comments on various points.

Criticisms and comments gleaned here and there will be brought before the group. There will be a discussion of the fairness or unfairness of these and what to do about them.

4. *The Order of Service*

The pastor is now ready to go over the orders of service for the Sunday or Sundays in question. He will present his thesis, purpose, aim, objective in whatever way he wishes to express it. Suggestions will be made concerning each item; discussion will follow; and the decision will be made. This is the time to discuss timing.

The pastor should ascertain the number of minutes required for the various musical items. Because of the nature of a certain program, it may be advisable and necessary at times to use the anthem as the offertory music. In some churches it is always so used. It should be kept in mind that self must be forgotten, and the personalities involved must bow to the spiritual needs of the hour. It is not a matter of each one getting his full time, but of making God real to the person in the pew.

At the close of this chapter several orders of service will be listed as examples of wise group planning.

5. *Long-Range Planning*

It is wise for the individuals to do some long-range planning; but it is also wise for the group to look ahead. Plans for Christmas, Easter, Mother's Day, and other special days need to be studied far in advance. Revival dates should be announced and plans started. Special music events, aside from regular worship services, should be discussed. What about the district music festival? How many choirs should go? What about transportation?

Choir camps and leadership conferences at Ridgecrest and Glorieta must be discussed many months in advance.

The participants, with more confidence in their work, will go away in a spirit of good will. Even more important is the solid program that has resulted from the meeting of hearts, minds, and talents.

III. REHEARSALS

No choir can make its maximum contribution to worship services without regularly scheduled rehearsals and consistent attendance on the part of choir members. Each element and procedure in the rehearsal should contribute to the choir member's spiritual and musical preparation.

1. *Why?*

Every choir, whether highly skilled or mediocre, can benefit from regularly scheduled rehearsals. Practice is essential, no matter how well trained the individual or the choir may be. Van Cliburn was once asked what he was doing during his stay at home. "Working," was his reply. "Doing what?" was the question. "Practicing on the piano," he said. When asked how much he practiced each day, he said that he spent eight hours at the piano. When surprise was expressed, he replied, "Other people work eight hours a day. This is my work. Why should I not spend eight hours at it?" This incident occurred about two years before he received international recognition.

Rehearsals are necessary not only to prepare the music for the coming worship services, but to build a spirit that will be contagious when the service is in progress. The more a group of people sing together, the more closely they are knit in heart and mind. Rehearsal affords a teaching opportunity such as nothing else affords.

2. How?

The "how" of the rehearsal is of great importance. Of course there is no set, unchangeable schedule. We can, however, make a few suggestions.

A wise procedure is to have the sopranos, altos, tenors, and basses meet in part sections to work on difficult anthems. A capable person from each section may be selected to serve as section leader. Nothing will build more confidence among the singers than these sectional practice sessions.

When the entire group assembles in the practice room or choir loft, it is wise to spend a few minutes discussing the successes or failures of the previous services. The criticism should be constructive.

The choir members have now had a brief respite and should be ready to sing. Practice briefly the musical portions of both services for the next Sunday. If the responses are not satisfactory, perfect them. If the hymns present problems, solve them immediately. Perfect the anthems! Do not slide over them in order to hurry to the cantata or oratorio that is still weeks away. By all means, be ready for Sunday.

When the Sunday services are well prepared, use the remaining time on future music, keeping several anthems in reserve. One choir director always rehearses eight anthems, keeping new ones flowing in as those used the previous Sunday are taken out. He divides the anthems roughly into four classes of two each, covering the light, the heavy, and those in between.

To allow a little rest for the voices, let the choir members engage in some theory contests and games. All musicians need to be refreshed in music theory. A good game is to have each person open his hymnal to the same number and take turns naming the key in which each hymn is written. Those who miss drop out. It is a spelling bee type of game, both interesting and helpful.

There are many such games. With the children's choirs a common one is to hold up flash cards with notes and music signs painted on them for identification. The entire choir can improve its sight reading by singing the scale as the director holds up any of eight fingers to indicate *do, re, mi*, etc.

The games over, there can be some final spirited singing before close of the period. Then the choir president will take charge to transact any business and to call for prayer.

3. When?

Many church choirs rehearse on Thursday night, while others use Wednesday night. In some instances, due to local conditions, it is necessary for the choir to use even another night for the rehearsal. Regardless of the night selected for choir rehearsal, it should be at a time when the choir members can attend and there is adequate time to prepare the music accurately.

It is evident that each church must use the time best suited to the schedules of the director, accompanists, and choir members. If preparation by the choir is neglected through the week, it almost goes without saying that it will be reflected in the music on Sunday.

Some few churches plan two rehearsals for the church choir, thus including more people. For example, one choir director meets with a smaller group on Tuesday night because they cannot attend on Thursday with the others. Then all are equally prepared on Sunday. Such an arrangement is good if it works!

It is fortunate for the church when the choir can have ten minutes together just prior to each worship service. It is so easy to forget important things the director pointed out on Thursday night. A brief period of refreshing is essential to the choir's best effort in the worship service.

The preservice warm-up is not a rehearsal! Never can ten minutes correct the loss of the hour or more of week-night preparation.

4. Where?

There are several places where choir rehearsals may be held. The best one is the place used by the choir on Sunday! Many choirs have suffered loss of effects because of the change from a low-ceiling practice room to the vaulted ceiling of the auditorium. Likewise, much has been lost when the piano was used in rehearsal and the organ in the actual service. The organist can best set up her stops and mark her copies at the rehearsal under the guidance of the music director.

Specially built choir rooms are good. Especially is it excellent to use them for teaching and for the preservice warm-up. If such facilities are available for the choir rehearsal, it is wise to move into the place of worship for the part of the practice period that is used to rehearse briefly the orders of service for Sunday.

It is expensive indeed to heat or cool the large auditorium

for a rehearsal. But the most expensive thing for a church is a poor program of worship.

5. *Who?*

In addition to the director and the accompanist, every member as well as every alternate member should be present. Some may not be ready for participation on Sunday. They may need weeks or months of training before they can take part in the worship services. Unfortunately, in many churches the need for choir strength is so great that there is no attempt to be selective. Fortunate is the church that has more choir members than seating space in the choir. It can then assign space to those who attend the rehearsals and also have persons in training for future service.

Some churches follow the procedure of maintaining an alternate list of choir members. In some instances these are persons who need additional training before becoming full-fledged members of the choir. With others, it is an arrangement where the maximum choir membership is set at a certain figure, and those beyond that number desiring membership in the choir serve as alternates until a vacancy occurs.

Such an arrangement may sound like big church business, but it is not. It can and should be used in any church!

On Sundays the director may wish to have one or two of the youth or children's choirs sing with the church choir. The usual procedure is to train them at their own rehearsal. A real effort must be made to get the various choirs together when especially difficult music is being planned. At least the few minutes before the service can be well used.

6. *Basic Instruction Needed*

Earlier in this discussion it was pointed out that the rehearsal time is a teaching time. Volunteer choirs are literally dotted with persons who possess good voices that are untrained.

The first large choir the author joined consisted of one hundred voices for each worship service with a large waiting list of aspiring young singers. The director spent a great deal of time at each rehearsal teaching sight reading and theory. Time so spent is never wasted! The time used in teaching will be more than compensated for by the readiness with which the choir learns new music.

Before leaving this study of rehearsals, let it be pointedly reiterated that the number one task of the minister of music is to prepare music for the worship services. All other work must take a lesser place even as the pastor must put everything else behind his work as a preacher and leader of worship. Be certain that the choir is able to sing the music well. Singing without adequate preparation is discouraging to the choir and of little value to the congregation.

IV. SPIRITUAL PREPARATION

Spiritual preparation is essential for the leader if he is to lead others in worship. Let us consider some of the ways those who lead can make such preparation.

1. *The Leaders*

All persons involved in worship leadership have the responsibility of being spiritually prepared. Each one should worship in private before attempting to lead others in public.

As in everything else, a plan is needed. Few will pray unless there is a deliberate plan and effort. Sermon preparation may result in a masterful essay or a dynamic gospel message. The manuscript can be the same; the difference lies in the heart of the preacher. So it is with the other leaders. Worshipfulness is contagious, infectious. If it is not evident in the leader, it will not be found among the people in the congregation.

Private worship is, then, a prime prerequisite. But what of the choir members?

2. *The Choir Members Too!*

The task of leading all the members of the choir to have private devotions just before gathering in the robing rooms or the practice room on Sunday is an impossible one. Some have been leading departments; others have been teaching classes or leading unions; still others have spent the previous hour figuring records. There has been no time for preparation except perhaps a few moments at home amid the rush of getting the family off to the church.

So, as important as the last minutes' tuning up is to the choir, even more necessary is the quiet moment of earnest prayer before taking their places in the choir. This is God's business. Never leave him out of the planning, the preparing, or the presenting of the worship program.

V. Suggested Orders of Service

The results of planning should be recorded. Orders of service should spring from the meeting of minds in the music conference. The pastor will complete them with the help of those he chooses and will get them ready for the printer. Here we see some of the fruits of a staff music conference.

1. *For Morning Worship*

(1)

"O Sing unto the Lord a new song. . . . shew forth his salvation from day to day" (Psalm 96:1–2)

Worship in Praise

Sacred Organ Music: "Faith of Our Fathers". . . .Arr. *McKinley*
Processional Hymn No. 417: "Lead On, O King Eternal". . *Smart*
Invocation
"Gloria Patri" (Choir and Congregation)
Anthem: "O Sing unto the Lord". . . . .*Hasler*
(The Church Choir)

Worship in Prayer

Reading of the Scriptures: Matthew 26: 36–46
Silent Meditation
Pastoral Prayer
Choral Response: "Hear Our Prayer, O Heavenly
    Father" ....*Chopin*

Worship in Giving

Recognitions
Hymn of Dedication No. 405: "Am I a Soldier of the
    Cross" ....*Arne*
Offertory: "Light Divine" ....*Gibbons-Willian*
Doxology
Offertory Prayer ....*The Assistant to the Pastor*

Worship in the Dedication of Life

Solo: "Be Still and Know"..........................*Bitgood*
Sermon: "THE DECISIVE BATTLEGROUND" (Matt. 26: 39)
    ....*The Pastor*
Hymn of Invitation No. 242:
    "Depth of Mercy! Can There Be".................*Weber*
Benediction and Choral Response
Organ Postlude: "Laudes Domini"...................*Wilson*

(2)

"Sing aloud unto God our strength: make a joyful noise
    unto the God of Jacob" (Psalm 81:1)

Organ Prelude: "Rest in the Lord".............*Mendelssohn*
Call to Worship: "Sanctus"........................*Norden*
Doxology
Invocation
Hymn No. 37: "Safely Through Another Week"........*Mason*
Recognitions
Scripture Reading: Responsive Reading No. 77
Prayer and Response

Hymn No. 118: "Majestic Sweetness Sits Enthroned"...*Hastings*

Offertory Prayer ....*The Youth Director*

Offertory: "Communion" ....*Purvis*

Anthem: "O Sing with the Angels"..................*Eichorn*

"O Saviour Sweet".........................*Bach*

"Jesus, Tender Shepherd".................*Dortch*

Sermon: "THE LORD'S DAY" (Ex. 20:3–6)..........*The Pastor*

Invitation Hymn No. 210: "I Lay My Sins on Jesus".....*Wesley*

Benediction and Response: "Amen".................*Lutkin*

Organ Postlude: "My Heart Ever Faithful".............*Bach*

(3)

"Be still and know that I am God: I will be exalted ...
in the earth" (Psalm 46:10)

Worship in Praise

Organ Prelude: "In Cruce Gloria"....................*Wilson*

Processional Hymn No. 56:
"Guide Me, O Thou Great Jehovah".............*Hastings*

Invocation

"Gloria Patri" (Choir and Congregation)

Anthem: "O Saviour Sweet"...........................*Bach*

(The Junior Choir)

Worship in Prayer

Reading of the Scriptures: Responsive Reading No. 37

Silent Meditation

Pastoral Prayer

Choral Response: "Hear Our Prayer, O Heavenly Father"
.... *Chopin*

Worship in Giving

Recognitions

Hymn of Dedication No. 367: "Take Time to Be Holy"..*Stebbins*

Doxology

Offertory Prayer..................*The Minister of Education*

Worship in the Dedication of Life

Anthem: "Laudamus Te"...........................*Mueller*
(The Church Choir)

Sermon: "Learning to Live Alone" (Psalm 27:10). *The Pastor*

Hymn of Invitation No. 355:
"Have Thine Own Way, Lord".................*Stebbins*

Benediction and Choral Response

Organ Postlude: "Saviour Victorious"................*Wilson*

(4)

The organ prelude is a veil dropped softly between the care-laden hours of the past week and the refreshing hour of worship. At the first sound of the organ, bow in silent prayer that God may speak to you.

Organ Prelude: "Solemn Melody".................*Schrieber*

Call to Worship

Hymn No. 21: "Welcome, Delightful Morn" ....*Schneider*
(As the organ music begins, the congregation is requested to rise and join in singing)

Invocation

"Gloria Patri" (Choir and Congregation)

Pastoral Prayer

Choral Response

Welcome to Visitors

Reading of the Scriptures

Hymn of Dedication No. 156: "Jesus, Lover of My Soul"..*Marsh*

Worship in Giving

Offertory: "Meditation" ....*Von Henselt*

Doxology

Anthem: "God Is Our Hope and Strength".............*Darst*
(The Church Choir)

Sermon: "When a Man Meets God" (Ex. 3:1-4)...*The Pastor*

Hymn of Invitation No. 243:
"I Am Coming to the Cross"....................*Fischer*

Benediction
Choral Response: "Saviour, Again to Thy Dear Name". . *Hopkins*
Organ Postlude: "Thou Art Repose". . . . . *Schubert*

(5)

Organ Prelude
Call to Worship: "O Worship the Lord". . . . . *McCutchan*
Invocation
Choral Response: "Fourfold Amen". . . . . *Stainer*
Hymn No. 2: "Love Divine, All Loves Excelling". . . . . . . *Zundel*
Hymn No. 150: "I Love Thee". . From Ingall's *Christian Harmony*
The Church Program. . . . . *The Pastor*
Hymn No. 400: "Something for Thee". . . . . *Lowry*
Offertory Prayer
Choral Response: "Bless Thou the Gifts". . . . . *Schumann*
Special Music: "O for a Thousand Tongues to Sing". . . . . *Jarman*
SERMON . . . . *The Pastor*
Invitation Hymn: "Jesus Calls Us o'er the Tumult". . . . . . . *Jude*
Choral Response: "The Lord Bless Thee and Keep Thee"
. . . . *McKinney*
Organ Postlude

2. For Evening Worship

(1)

Organ Prelude: "Prayer". . . . . *Franck*
Call to Worship: "The Old Rugged Cross". . . . . *Bennard*
Hymn No. 207: "Rescue the Perishing". . . . . *Doane*
Hymn No. 155: "Jesus Is All the World to Me". . . . . . *Thompson*
Prayer
Announcements and Recognition of Visitors
Hymn No. 174: "Breathe on Me". . . . . *McKinney*
Offertory: "One Sweetly Solemn Thought". . . . . *Ambrose*
Anthem: "Into the Woods My Master Went". . . . . *Lutkin*
Sermon: "RESISTING GOD'S SPIRIT" (Acts 7:51–60)
. . . . *The Pastor*

Invitation Hymn No. 218:
"While We Pray and While We Plead"..............*Case*
Benediction and Response:
"Jesus, Keep Me Near the Cross"...............*Doane*
Organ Postlude: "Hymn-Medley"..............Arr. *Birdsong*

(2)

Organ Prelude: "O God, Thou Good God"..........*Karg-Elert*
Call to Worship: "O Jesus, Thou Art Standing"..*Knecht-Husband*
Hymn No. 29: "Day Is Dying in the West"............*Sherwin*
Hymn No. 143: "I Will Sing of My Redeemer"....*McGranahan*
Announcements and Recognition of Visitors
Hymn No. 97: "Jesus, Keep Me Near the Cross"........*Doane*
Offertory: "Sabbath Melody".......................*Mueller*
Anthem: "Welsh Choral".......................*Reese-Jones*
Sermon: "SPIRITUAL SUICIDE" (John 5:40)........*The Pastor*
Invitation Hymn No. 230:
"Let Jesus Come into Your Heart"................*Morris*
Benediction and Response: "Our God Is Watching"....*Lovelace*
Organ Postlude: "Postlude"........................*Wagner*

(3)

Organ Prelude: "Psalm XIX"......................*Marcello*
Choral Call to Worship No. 13:
"All People That on Earth Do Dwell"..........*Bourgeois*
Invocation
Ordinance of Baptism
Gospel Song Service ....*Minister of Music*
Recognition of Visitors
Announcements
Hymn No. 56: "Guide Me, O Thou Great Jehovah"....*Hastings*
The Evening Offering
Organ Offertory: "Prayer" ("Finlandia")............*Sibelius*
Choral Worship: "Christ Triumphant"............*Pietro Yon*
Message: "THE DEAD LIVE AGAIN" (March 5:22–24). *The Pastor*

Hymn of Invitation No. 237: "Lord, I'm Coming Home"
.... *Kirkpatrick*
Benediction
Organ Postlude: "Marche" .... *Guilmant*

(4)

Organ Prelude
Hymn No. 253: "Have Faith in God"............. *McKinney*
Hymn No. 283 "The Solid Rock".................. *Bradbury*
Prayer
Hymn No. 52: "O Love of God Most Full"............ *Jackson*
The Church Program
Hymn No. 369: "Purer in Heart, O God"............ *Fillmore*
Special Music: "I Heard the Voice of Jesus Say"........ *Dykes*
SERMON .... *The Pastor*
Invitation Hymn: "Take My Life, and Let It Be"........ *Malan*
Benediction
Choral Response: "God Be with You"................. *Tomer*
Organ Postlude

All hymns indicated are from *Baptist Hymnal*.

FOR FURTHER STUDY AND DISCUSSION

1. Check with your librarian, your pastor, and your minister of music for books on the work of the pastor and the minister of music. Ask also for books on planning worship services. These will increase your appreciation of the work of these ministers.
2. If at the close of chapter 5 you did not make out several orders of service, be sure to do so now. Be careful of each step. Use variety. Be careful of balance. Show your work to your pastor.

CHAPTER 8 OUTLINE

I. THE STATED SERVICES

II. SPECIAL DAYS

III. PUBLIC CEREMONIES

IV. REVIVAL MEETINGS

8

Music for Special Services

IT IS IMPERATIVE that the worship service of Christian groups be permeated with spiritual meaning. Thought and care in the selection of the music will contribute to the pleasure, instruction, and inspiration of any group of worshipers, young or old.

I. THE STATED SERVICES

In most of our churches the calendar of activities is carefully set so far as worship services are concerned. On Sunday there is always morning worship. Evening services are almost as certain in Baptist churches, but are growing less common among other groups. The midweek prayer meeting service too is customary among Baptists. Some of the other denominations have discarded it.

There are many special events each year, most of which are observed on Sunday. These should receive careful attention by those who plan the music program of the church. In order to cover the field adequately we shall deal with the various types of public worship service.

1. *Morning Worship*

Many churches have found it advisable, even necessary, to have two morning services. This poses a real problem. The extra burden falls not only on the preacher, but on the musicians as well. The choir director is invariably involved. Unless the church is blessed with several accompanists, the same organist and pianist must serve at both worship hours.

The choirs are often divided to share the services. Usually a youth choir sings at the early service. Often ensembles and soloists assist with the early worship service. Reports show that in some cases the eight-thirty service has outgrown the eleven-o'clock service. Our business is to reach people. If we can serve more of them by having the extra worship period, it is good to plan and promote it.

As has been said before, the morning worship service usually moves with more precision. Often a time limitation is responsible for this. The hymns, anthems, responses, solos, and all other selections should be chosen wisely and with the greatest care. Appropriate instrumental music should fit into the order of service with perfect timing.

This is primarily a worship service! Every possible means should be used to reach the heart of each individual.

2. Evening Worship

The evening service, as we have pointed out before, is usually less formal and more spirited. The singing majors on gospel songs that have life and vigor. Such freedom opens the door for a variety of musical numbers such as solos, duets, trios, quartets, ensembles, instrumental solos. There is usually greater warmth, and the evangelistic spirit runs high. Wherever such is not true, the attendance is usually small, the people scattered, and the results negative.

Truly the evening service offers the best opportunity to emphasize something "special." It should be planned as such, advertised as such, and then carried out as promised. To build up interest and then fail to follow through is to invite failure.

3. Midweek Prayer Meeting Service

Some churches are well known for the success of their prayer meeting. The "Hour of Power" emphasis has been exceedingly successful in many churches. Music is not necessarily the major emphasis, but it does have its place. In fact, the service is undergirded by the same type of music one expects on Sunday night.

One of the best opportunities for participation of the graded choirs is on Wednesday night. It should be made clear, however, that the singing of the younger choirs is to be in line with the worship emphasis—not merely an interesting performance for the gratification of parents.

We cannot believe that people "just will not attend prayer meeting." The failure is sometimes a direct reflection on the leadership.

4. *Worship in the Educational Organizations*

Both Sunday school and Training Union organizations use a great deal of music in their assemblies, in which the worship of God is the main purpose. In them there is always group singing, and often special musical numbers have a part in making an attractive, helpful program. The use of graded choirs in the assembly programs is discouraged because it takes the participants from their regular age-group departments. Now is a good time to stress the danger of taking children out of their classes and unions for a musical program, even the morning or evening service. If they know they are to leave early, they will not concentrate on the lesson or program of their own department.

Every group in the church organization that meets for a program of worship uses music. The WMS and its auxiliaries, the Brotherhood, the Royal Ambassadors—all have a place for music. Every organization benefits when there is an adequate church music program. Surely, a meeting of minds in church leadership is necessary for the desired curriculum correlation.

II. Special Days

Music for special occasions or services in our churches should be selected with the utmost care. Since there is such a scarcity of excellent materials in certain areas, worship leaders must be sure to avoid overuse or too frequent duplication.

Because of the very nature of these special services music can add much to their effectiveness.

1. *The Lord's Supper*

Unanimity is lacking in Baptist churches in the observance of the Lord's Supper both as to time and form. No statistical survey has been made, but it is likely that the majority of them observe the Lord's Supper quarterly. Next in order is the monthly, and then the semi-annual, observance. So far as we know, no Baptist church uses the service weekly.

The place in the worship service is also subject to the policies of the local church or, more often, the desire of the leader. Most of our churches observe the Lord's Supper at the close of a morning or an evening service. Some have found it far better to place it at the very center of the worship hour. Such a practice keeps it from seeming like an appendage, which often runs beyond the usual time, causing unrest among the people. Unrest is never conducive to worship. The author has found it helpful to place the observance of the Supper just prior to the anthem and sermon. Through careful planning, the entire morning service is kept within one hour without giving the impression of haste.

The Lord's Supper, when rightly observed, offers one of the best opportunities for worship. The entire service, beginning with the prelude, should deal with the suffering of our Lord: the garden, the thorns, the cross, the blood. With wise selection and planning the organist can arrange a musical background consisting of familiar hymns portraying the suffering of Jesus.

The worship leader may read Bible passages, poems, or hymns related to the subject. All of this is especially necessary when the service is broadcast. Leaders should keep in mind the blessing that shut-ins may receive from such a service by radio. The choir (while seated) may even sing softly some of the songs that fit the serving of the bread or the fruit of the vine.

It is our firm conviction that many people stay away from church on days when the Lord's Supper is to be served simply because their experience with such services has been unsatisfactory. Let music have its proper place. Make the whole service a rich and satisfying experience in which well-trained deacons carry out their assignments reverently and flawlessly.

Some pastors plan, now and then, to use the entire hour for the Lord's Supper, omitting the usual sermon. Surely the way is open for great variety. One should keep in mind the seriousness of the matter and the effectiveness of good music in such an experience.

Among the hymns most acceptable for this service are: " 'Tis Midnight and on Olive's Brow," "Alas, and Did My Saviour Bleed," "Into the Woods My Master Went," "When I Survey the Wondrous Cross," "There Is a Fountain," "Here, O My Lord," "Here at Thy Table, Lord," "Bread of the World, in Mercy Broken," "Bread of Heav'n, on Thee We Feed," "Be Known to Us in Breaking Bread."

Some of these are not as well known as they should be, and therefore are often omitted. If, however, they are first read by the minister and then sung by the choir, the people will be able to recognize them when the organist plays them as background music. They can thus enrich the worship experience.

Anthems that exactly fit the Lord's Supper are not as plentiful as we could wish. Some favorites are: "At Thy Table, Lord," A. Floyd; "Be Still My Soul," C. H. Kitson; "Bread of the World," H. B. Gaul; "I Am the Bread of Life," J. S. Matthews; "O Bread of Life," F. M. Christiansen; "O Living Bread, Who Once Did Die," P. W. Whitlock. There are many usable anthems on the theme of love, the cross, the sacrifice, and many excellently arranged hymn-anthems. One should consult *The Church Musician* constantly for the best in this field. Many of the anthems may be ordered individually.

2. *Baptism*

The other church ordinance is baptism. Most Baptist churches observe it during the evening service, some preferring the beginning of the hour, others the closing period. Rarely do ministers baptize during the morning worship hour. At least once each year it is good to have both baptism and the Lord's Supper at the same service with a message on the ordinances.

In this service also there is opportunity for both beauty and meaning. Appropriate dress, lighting, Scripture reading, and music should be used. The choir may open the baptismal service with an appropriate hymn. The organist will then play softly while the candidate for baptism is entering the pool and is being placed under the water. At that point the organist may gradually increase the volume to express victory. No better hymn can be found than "He Arose." It is perfectly suited for the service because of the naturally quiet stanza followed by the naturally vigorous refrain, "Up from the grave He arose."

Hymns for the baptismal service are few indeed. The ones available are not very familiar to us. It is evident that special care needs to be exercised because of the small number of songs from which to select the ones needed for an effective service. A new one is "This Rite Our Blest Redeemer Gave." It is in the *Baptist Hymnal.* Another unfamiliar one is "Come, Holy Spirit, Dove Divine." Others usually listed, and more familiar are: "O Jesus, I Have Promised," "Jesus, I My Cross Have Taken," and "O Thou Who in Jordan."

Anthems on the subject of baptism are just as few or fewer than the hymns. Unfortunately for Baptists, the catalogs of many music publishers list mostly anthems featuring infant baptism. For example, one list of six selections under the heading of "Baptism," contains only two that do not mention "little children." Although we now baptize many boys and girls who may be called little children, it does not seem wise to include such anthems in our repertoire.

3. *National Holidays*

There are many special days listed on the calendars each year. Some of them, such as the birthdays of great men, are given slight, if any, recognition by the churches. Others, however, receive major attention by most of us. These are Mother's Day, Father's Day, Memorial Day, Independence Day, Labor Day, Veterans' Day, and Thanksgiving. Each offers an opportunity to capitalize on current thinking.

It is not always advisable to plan the entire service around the special day, but it is wise to occasionally give it recognition. A good example is Mother's Day. It is next to impossible to preach an effective Mother's Day sermon every year. The subject, though a beautiful one, is limited. Proper recognition may be given through the use of a special bulletin, introduction of the oldest and newest mothers, the one having borne the most children. Or the day may be recognized through a proper emphasis in organ music, solo, or anthem.

It is of vital importance to remember that despite the popularity of the special day, Sunday is the Lord's Day! The service is one of worship. God in Christ is ever the central theme. No war hero, no statesman, no victory in battle, not even mother, should take the spotlight away from the gospel.

Good hymnals provide several hymns which fit the patriotic theme. There are five listed in the *Baptist Hymnal* and seven in *The Broadman Hymnal*. During the last decade the favorite has been "Mine Eyes Have Seen the Glory." Some stirring arrangements of it have been published. Another favorite is the brilliant "God of Our Fathers, Whose Almighty Hand." It serves as an excellent processional hymn.

The anthem writers too have made a real contribution to the patriotic music for church services. Many church libraries contain "America the Beautiful," H. R. Shelley; "Anthem of Democracy," J. H. Matthews; "God Save America," W. F. Harling; "Land of Hope and Glory," E. Elgar; "O God of Freedom," E. S. Barnes; "Our United States," L. Stokowski; and "Recessional," R. de Koven.

Much of the vocal literature is also usable as organists' preludes, offertories, and postludes.

Since Thanksgiving is more of a religious than patriotic occasion, it is natural that there should be a much wider selection of music. Moreover, the Bible affords abundant material for Scripture readings and sermons on the theme of gratitude to God. The *Baptist Hymnal* lists ten Thanksgiving hymns, and choir manuals feature anthems too numerous to list here. Despite this fact, some church choirs insist on using the same anthems every year. Some excellent anthems are "Psalm of Thanksgiving," J. H. Maunder; "A Prayer of Thanksgiving," E. Kremser; "A Psalm of Gratitude," C. W. Cadman.

4. Religious "Festivals"

Perhaps the word *festival* is not the best one. But it is a commonly used one! Those churches which regularly give emphasis to special days of the church year will observe more than the two festivals we shall name. We are to deal only with our Lord's birth (Christmas) and his resurrection (Easter). The latter is usually expanded to include the entire passion of Jesus Christ. For both of these there are hymns, anthems, solos, and organ pieces by the hundreds.

Let us consider Christmas music first. The increasing commercialism causes the old songs to blare forth from horns and speakers all over the towns and to come from radios and television sets until people grow weary of them.

It is wise for the churches to use them less frequently but

more carefully. Make them really special! The *Baptist Hymnal* lists twenty hymns under the "Birth of Christ." There is a wise mixing of the less familiar with the old revered ones.

Christmas is a season of deep and joyous meaning. The church services should express this joy. From the first note of the prelude to the last one of the postlude let the joy bells peal forth. Use every choir during the season. Plan a carol and candle lighting service. Sing a cantata. Do something thrilling and outstanding. Sing carols. Sing hymns. Sing anthems. Let all the people sing at Christmas time!

Most of the things we have said of Christmas are also true of Easter. The music is plentiful. It is a season of joy. The season will open with Palm Sunday. Wise leaders will not miss this opportunity. A brilliant solo is in order. Some good ones are: "Open the Gates of the Temple," Knapp; "Hosanna," J. Granier; "Jerusalem," H. Parker. Good music is available also for choirs and organists.

If no special service is held during the week to point to the death of Christ on the cross, use Sunday night after the Palm Sunday emphasis of that morning.

The effectiveness of the Easter service will depend largely on the vivid portrayal of the suffering and death of Jesus. The Wednesday night service, if properly planned and publicized, can be made as effective as a Sunday service. Eighteen hymns are listed in the *Baptist Hymnal* under "His Suffering and Death." They are among our most familiar songs.

Easter dawns as the day of days for most Christians. Those who seldom attend church make a special effort on this day. We must make the most of it! Rather than remind those who seldom come that they are derelict in their Christian duty, we must make the day so challenging, so spiritual, so helpful that they will want to return again and again.

Easter is a day of music. Whether it is a sunrise service or the eleven o'clock hour, music is expected to play an important role in the Christian's observance of the occasion. Exultant, joyous music marks Easter services. The sermon should be brief, pointed, challenging. Brevity seldom cripples a sermon. More time and effort are required for preparation of a brief sermon. But it is worthy of the minister's best. *The Crucifixion* and *The Seven Last Words* are past. The glory of the resurrection now demands "Hymn Exultant," J. W. Clokey; "Alleluia! Christ Is Risen," A. Kopyloff; and others.

If music is ever to be predominant in services of worship, it should be in the great Christian festivals, Christmas and Easter.

III. PUBLIC CEREMONIES

The two public ceremonies most common in the churches are weddings and funerals. Either service may be held elsewhere. There was a time when both funerals and weddings were commonly held in the home. Now, however, wedding ceremonies are more often performed in the pastor's home, his study, a church parlor, church chapel, or church auditorium.

Funeral services are now held most often in the space provided by the funeral home or in the church building—chapel or auditorium.

1. *Weddings*

Public weddings invariably give music an important place in the entire service. The organ is used not only for accompanying soloists, but for providing the music before and after the ceremony. Quite often the ceremony is made more impressive by the playing of very soft background music.

The wedding affords an excellent opportunity to exert a Christian influence upon the wedding party and all those in attendance. The greatest impact should be made by the minister in the wedding ceremony with his carefully chosen words of counsel, vows, and prayers.

Of equal importance is the music. Since the wedding is a sacred occasion, it deserves the highest type of sacred music. On two recent occasions, the author heard "Saviour, Like a Shepherd Lead Us" sung at weddings. It was most effective. "The Lord's Prayer" and "O Perfect Love" are frequently used, especially at the close of the ceremony.

Since it has become traditional for the bride to select her wedding music, many a conscientious church musician has quailed before the requests made. Yet the average bride has no intention of disregarding the sanctity of the church when she selects her wedding music.

Frequently the bride is not a musical person, or she has not developed an appreciation for the better class of music. It is possible that a bride may be so overwhelmed with the details of the happy event that she gives insufficient thought to the music. It is easy for her to decide to use the same music that a close friend used at her wedding, with utter disregard as to suitability and appropriateness.

The church musician can do much to help the bride select music that is reverent. A kindly discussion with the bride and groom concerning the purpose of music for a wedding usually results in a more careful and more prayerful consideration of the selections to be used.

What music is appropriate for a Christian wedding?

Apply this simple test: Are the words of the song such that the pastor would find appropriate to quote as part of a wedding service? If the minister performing the wedding ceremony would not find those words suitable, what right has a soloist to use them there?

One needs to guard against the so-called popular love songs that should have no place in a Christian wedding. They do not fit the Christian concept of marriage! The right choice in music, we repeat, is as important as the right choice of words for the ceremony.

2. *Funerals*

There is no shortage of good music for funerals. The good, standard hymnals are the best sources from which to choose the music. Generally, organ books provide no help. Familiar music should be used. Therefore, lean heavily on the hymns.

Unfortunately the cheap, paper-back songbooks have crept into funeral services just as they have in church services. The wise minister will gently lead the family away from these. The minister or the music director, if he is asked, can wield a strong influence for good in this area.

In many instances, the organist or pianist has the burden of responsibility for the funeral music. Sometimes choirs, quartets, and soloists sing, but the vast majority of services, especially in the cities and larger towns, use only instrumental music. The music should be designed to comfort and console the saddened family. Most vocal music affects the emotions deeply, causing outbursts of weeping.

The funeral affords an unusual opportunity to give a true Christian testimony. As in the wedding, the music is as important as the words of the minister. Therefore, it is necessary to plan the services with the greatest wisdom and sympathy.

IV. REVIVAL MEETINGS

Great revivals have always been characterized by powerful and persuasive singing. The right kind of music properly used in a revival has often been used of the Holy Spirit to bring conviction and spiritual blessing to the unregenerated.

1. *How They Differ*

The revival service is very much like the usual evening service in most churches, with more singing and a more urgent invitation. The people have been prepared for an emotional appeal. Time is not uppermost in the minds of the people. They expect to stay longer.

More than any other one thing, the impact of successive days and nights of revival keeps the interest high and the work effective. It is, as folk used to say, a "protracted meeting."

When considering the differences between revival meetings and other meetings, we think first of the new faces and new voices. Revivals bring in visiting preachers and song leaders. Often they are specialists in the field of evangelism. There is pulling power in the term, "evangelist." The people will accept statements from the visiting minister that a local worker could not make without causing trouble. So also they will accept music leadership with the use of wind instruments and other unusual devices that would not be acceptable in the regular worship services. The revival meeting is different; it is special; it is a Baptist distinctive.

2. *Music in the Revival*

The music used in a revival must have dignity of purpose if it is to be effective in bringing spiritual blessings to the people. It must be music with a message, appealing to the unsaved and pointing them to the Saviour.

(1) *The value of music.*—It has been stated again and again that music in worship is essential. Congregational singing, almost lost during the Dark Ages, was revived with the Reformation and was further developed by Calvin, the Wesleys, Whitefield, Jonathan Edwards, and others. Since that period, it has increased steadily. In worship services it is never satisfactory to let a few people sing for many. If this principle is true in a worship service, it is even more of a requirement in evangelistic services.

If you have attended a worship service led by Billy Graham and his associates, you know that although there is much emphasis on special musical numbers, the major music force is in the congregation. It takes the singing of all the people to make the service a victorious one—great choir, splendid accompaniments, heart-moving solos, congregational participation.

In revival meetings music creates "atmosphere." Dwight L. Moody was not a singer, but it was his conviction that even if the sermon was below par, the great singing would move the hearts. The preacher himself is usually moved to greater preaching by the music of the service. Music does prepare the way! Not only does it open the door—often it is the door.

(2) *The song leader.*—One reason for the growing demand for specialists in the music field of evangelism is the realization that song leadership is too important to be taken lightly. The song leader is a specialist. He is a part of a team dealing with the souls of men. His musicianship should be sound, his spirit good, his personality acceptable. A good solo voice will be a real asset, but it is not an absolute essential.

The qualifications of the song leader have been listed by various writers. The order may vary, but the qualifications remain the same. They are: Christian character, loyal church member, good personality, a pleasing speaking voice, neat personal appearance, a co-operative spirit, a sense of humor, humility, knowledge of music. It was dealt with earlier, and the revivalist in the music field needs to know no less than the church music director.

It should be kept in mind that the song leader needs to be a fluent speaker in order to say effectively what needs to be said; but he does not need to talk much. A long story of a hymn may be of consuming interest to the song leader, but rarely will a group of people share that interest.

Beware of tricks. Perhaps you have been in a service where the song leader led the people to place their hands to their mouths like trumpets to increase the volume. One leader had the people to lean far to the right and then to the left while singing "Leaning on Jesus." Such stunts do not create a worshipful atmosphere, but tend rather to cheapen the singing and destroy the spiritual meaning of the song.

(3) *The accompanists.*—Both organ and piano should be used when they are available. Both the organist and the pianist need to follow the same set of rules, or guiding principles. They are both positive and negative.

On the positive side are the following: Understand that the director is the interpreter of the music. Follow him. Play introductions without dragging. End introductions with the tonic chord. Play the chords as written without great embellishment. Be prompt. Be co-operative. Practice!

On the negative side are rules which, in some instances, are covered by the positive statements: Never drag. Do not "fill in" unless highly skilled in doing so, and then sparingly! Do not change the harmonic structure when accompanying congregational singing. Do not change organ registrations during the playing of a hymn except in rare cases.

(4) *The revival choir.*—Briefly, the revival choir is little different from the regular choir. Because anthems are seldom used in revivals, it is possible to increase the choir, allowing more youth and inexperienced singers to enter. There is real value in having every seat filled. The congregation has need of the strong leading of a full choir.

In some churches there is a feeling that the choir should not be robed during the week-night services. This may be right, but the use of robes is now so common that the failure to use them may cause more comment than would the formality of a robed choir. The many-colored dresses and shirts can hardly add to the evangelistic fervor! The leader will handle this matter with caution and wisdom.

(5) *The type of music used.*—What is revival music? Usually it is little different from the warm, evangelistic Sunday evening service with which we are all familiar. The difference lies in the increase of quantity and the accumulative impact.

The gospel songs are more often used in revival services than are the majestic hymns of worship and praise. There are, however, some notable exceptions, such as "All Hail the Power of Jesus' Name," "When I Survey the Wondrous Cross," "Crown Him with Many Crowns," "Holy Ghost, with Light Divine."

There is always the danger of overdoing the gospel song approach. The temptation is to race and almost "swing" some of the songs. Great care should be exercised at this point.

Special music is widely used and effective in the revival. Often the gospel can be presented better by the soloist than by the choir because the words are more easily understood. Now and then a truly exceptional soloist can sing "big" numbers effectively. "The Penitent," "If with All Your Hearts," and "The Lord Is My Light" are good examples. However, the heart-moving song in the hymnal or solo book will more often be acceptable. The other extreme is to be avoided at all times, that of using the so-called sacred song "swing style" made popular on juke boxes and television programs.

3. *Worship in Evangelism*

We must not close this chapter without making it clear that evangelism does not exclude worship. Too often it has done so to the hurt of true evangelism.

Here the burden of the responsibility falls on the song leader inasmuch as he is usually conducting the service. It is his privilege, in co-operation with the pastor and the evangelist, to plan a broad program of worship in music. It is our deep conviction that evangelism will be more fruitful if the worship atmosphere is created early in the service. It is God and not the evangelist who is in the center. Strive to help the person in the pew to encounter God in Christ, long before the sermon is preached.

FOR FURTHER STUDY AND DISCUSSION

1. Attend services morning, evening, and on Wednesday night. Make careful notes on all three. Mark the similarities; the differences. Which was the best planned? Which meant most to you?
2. When the Lord's Supper is served, pay special attention to each detail. What music is used? Be alert to what is played on the organ. Examine yourself as to your awareness of Christ and his sacrifice for you.
3. Plan definitely to be present at a baptismal service, a wedding, a funeral. Study each in the light of your work in this book.
4. Try to attend every service of the next revival meeting. Be a close observer and an active participant.

CHAPTER 9 OUTLINE

9

Aids to the Improvement of Public Worship

THE SKILL of a builder can usually be determined by the quality and condition of his tools. First, he must make a wise selection of equipment. However, regardless of skill in selectivity of tools, they are of little value unless he is agile in the use of them and gives them proper care.

The "tools of worship" are no exception. Only the best should be used. And anything that merits use even one time may be used again in the future. Therefore, it should be acquired and maintained with such a purpose.

I. EQUIPMENT

It is true that one can worship God anywhere. But it is also true that some places and some situations are more conducive to worship than others. To make it easier for people to worship God in spirit and in truth a church should provide the best possible surroundings and leadership.

1. *The Building*

The meeting place for worship is important. A brush arbor is acceptable only if there is no better place. The little one-room frame church house will suffice if nothing else can be provided. The building does make a difference.

Therefore, careful attention should be given to the building. "But we already have our building. We are not pleased, but what can we do about it?" There is a great deal you can do about it. If it is important enough to you, you can lay carpets, rearrange furnishings and equipment, redecorate, remodel, add lights, soften lights, etc. One church tore out the unattractive baptistry with its amateur painting and built a new one of beauty and grace. It was the one change that was needed.

Although a church may have no plans for remodeling its present physical facilities, it can keep the building clean and uncluttered. Dirt in God's house is a disgrace to all who share the responsibility.

If you are planning to have a new building in the near future, be sure to study the plans for the auditorium to make sure it is worshipful. The lighting is important. So is sound. Quietness is essential. Too often we are more interested in the number of people a building will seat than in whether or not it is conducive to worship.

2. *Arrangements*

The building itself is of such great importance that extreme care should be taken in planning the new one or remodeling the old. Of almost equal importance, however, is the arrangement within the building. Lighting, which we have discussed, will mean more if there is something of beauty and worshipfulness to make it effective. The furniture, for example, should be of good quality and well placed. In most churches flowers can be arranged every week. If fresh flowers are not available, there are some very nice artificial plants and flowers that may be used. By all means, do not clutter walls. Keep them as attractive as you can.

Not all churches can have stained-glass windows, but their windows can be kept sparkling clean and unbroken. Even tinting can be done easily now. It cuts down glare and adds dignity.

3. *Organ and/or Piano*

Almost every church can afford an organ. The small ones are about equal in price to a grand piano. The most common arrangement in Baptist churches is to have the organ and the piano on opposite sides of the pulpit in direct view of the music director's podium.

There are some older buildings that still have the organ console against the wall behind the choir where the organist must see everything with a rearview mirror. Possibly there are those who wonder who thought of such a plan in the first place. The practice actually originated with the development of the tracker action organ, necessitating the need to place the console near the organ. This type of organ action is rare in this country today. It has become almost obsolete during the past two decades.

Whether a church can afford large expensive instruments or not, the ones they have should, by all means, be kept in good condition. Tuners can be employed to give regular service for a prearranged flat fee plus any materials used for the repairs. In the author's church the organ tuner comes twice each year when the change is made from heating to air conditioning and back again to heating. The piano tuner tunes and repairs all pianos twice annually.

Surely it is not out of place here to say that it is good for the instruments to be used. Guard them carefully against abuse, but let them be played. Some organs are now made with open consoles having no lock or key. The president of one company said, "Let people play it; that is what it was made for." If students do not have access to instruments for practice, our churches will be the losers.

4. *Robes*

Nothing has helped more to make choir robes popular than has the advent of graded choirs. Now almost any church can robe a choir without even one member resigning! Robes are expensive initially, but if properly cared for they will last many years. If possible there should be a change of robes. If not, then a different-colored stole will help. As the old robes begin to show wear, purchase new ones, and change colors from time to time. If the first ones were black, try white or maroon or blue. Let a color expert decide what will look best in the choir loft. If the color is not right now, it may be better to paint the area around the choir than to buy new robes.

Again maintenance is important. Use deodorants. Hang the robes carefully. If the space for them is open, use a cover for them. Have them cleaned when they need it.

II. Materials

A craftsman is often judged by the quality of the tools and materials used in his trade. This is no less true of the minister of music. The right kind of materials constitute an effective "liaison" between music leaders and those they enlist and train.

1. *Literature*

Few churches skimp on literature for Sunday school, Training Union, and the other organizations. There is no reason why the Music Ministry should suffer. *The Church Musician,* Southern Baptists' splendid music magazine, is as necessary for the music director, accompanists, and choir members as the quarterly is for the pupils in Sunday school.

The church may also subscribe to other music periodicals for the minister of music, accompanists, and other music leaders.

2. *Hymnals*

Good hymnals are needed in every room where public services are held. The Sunday School Board (Broadman and

Convention Press) makes available hymnals suitable for all areas of church work. The most recent is *Baptist Hymnal*. A common practice is to thrust the old books into departments of the various organizations when new hymnals are purchased for the church auditorium. This is not bad if the books are of acceptable quality and in usable condition and if they are placed in departments for Adults and Young People.

3. *Anthems*

Every music director should have several anthem catalogs and should be on the mailing list of several music publishers. Among these should be the *Baptist Book Store Catalog* which always includes a complete listing of Broadman choral music along with a listing of current releases of other publishers.

Only a few years are required to build up a good choir library. It is wise to order sample copies first. If the full order is placed without careful study, the library is soon filled with useless material. If a request is made early for an increase in the music budget, it is seldom refused. It is important that church leaders know the minister of music is not wasteful.

The Church Musician not only provides many anthems and hymn arrangements for churches of various sizes, but it is full of helpful information covering the whole church music field.

4. *Teaching Materials*

The director of music needs many tools. He is a craftsman. Each age group calls for something different. As a teacher of music he must have the usual instruments and will find helpful the following ones for use with the younger choirs: Autoharp, metal bars, triangles, rhythm sticks, Indian drums, flutophones, plastic octave bells, etc.

One of the essentials is a tape recorder. Here again is the problem of expense, but this is not the place to economize. This machine can be used in many different ways. Even the adults need it so that they may have the amazing, and often disappointing, experience of hearing themselves sing. A small portable machine can be used not only by the Music Ministry but in almost every phase of church activity.

A good record player is also an asset. You can use it to demonstrate the fine quality singing by great music groups, thus challenging your own choir's abilities. It is important for them to compare their own productions with those of choirs and choral groups which have reached the top rung of the musical ladder.

For the younger graded choirs *The Baptist Book Store Catalog* lists only those materials that have been carefully appraised and recommended for those groups.

Among the teaching materials one should use are books, magazines, flash cards, opaque projectors, and many other items in addition to musical instruments. If a good place is made for their care and keeping they will be usable for many years.

5. *The Music Library*

The music library is the depository for both music and the books needed in a church music program. Ample space needs to be provided and proper shelving supplied.

A system for filing the anthems, as well as other music materials, should be adopted. For music library materials procure the free pamphlet, *The Church Music Record System,* from your state music secretary or from the Church Music Department, Baptist Sunday School Board. It is helpful to have a large collection of hymnals and books for men's and women's voices for use on special occasions.

If the church has a library, a music section should be maintained. The section may include general books which the music leaders could check out as needed. A complete set of music texts in the Church Study Course for Teaching and

Training should be included in this section. The minister of music should work closely with the librarian in developing this part of the library. Frequent reference to the *Baptist Book Store Catalog* for listings of new materials will prove useful in expanding this section.

A faithful choir member is usually willing to serve as music librarian. He may need an assistant. Many choirs include such officers as a part of their choir organization. The director will probably have him to distribute, collect, and replace all items used at rehearsals. Choir sponsors can help with such tasks at rehearsals of younger choirs.

III. THE MUSIC TRAINING PROGRAM

If we will put forth as much effort in the Music Ministry as has been used in our other church organizations to provide trained workers, effective leadership will become the usual rather than the exceptional part of a progressive church Music Ministry.

1. *Church Music Schools*

In the Sunday school and Training Union it is necessary to have periodic teaching and training emphases. In the Music Ministry of the church the need for a teaching and training emphasis is equally important. There are several approaches. The first is the regular schedule of classes and rehearsals for all age groups.

The second approach is the study course plan. Music leaders should acquaint themselves with the Church Study Course for Teaching and Training and proceed to organize a training program in co-operation with other leaders of the church. Such a program, over a period of time, will assure the church of trained leaders for all areas of the Music Ministry. Such a study challenges not only choir members but many other people in the church. There is a growing list of good books keeping pace with the increasing interest in the church music program.

Always we face the money problem in the church program. If it is impossible to secure outside help, enlist local talent. But money spent in bringing in a challenging faculty is good economy.

The third approach is the choir camp. In the June, 1959, issue of *The Church Musician* (pp. 63–64), there is a helpful article about the "Summer Music Day Camp." The author tells of the disappointment his group experienced when the scheduled music camp was cancelled. Immediately he set about to remedy the situation by conducting day camps at home. Using the spacious choir room and all the equipment at hand, he brought the Primary group together for morning camp and the Juniors for afternoon camp. There were thirty campers in each group. There was first a devotional period, followed by a vocal warm-up and technique session, the teaching of a study course text, recreation, singing, workbook time, refreshments and recess, hymn singing and hymnology, rhythm sticks and musical games, flutophone orchestra, study of the modern symphony, cleanup time, and dismissal. The morning group stayed from 8:30 until 11:00, and the afternoon group from 2:00 until 4:30.

2. *Special Classes*

The minister of music who directs a fully-graded Music Ministry has little time to give private instruction. The organist may be able to take a few students. The special class provides an opportunity for unusual learning privileges for vocalists and instrumentalists. That which can be taught an individual can usually be taught a group of individuals. Because of time limitations, no choir can do all that needs to be done during rehearsal. Special classes for both vocalists and instrumentalists will therefore be profitable to the students and to the church. Piano classes in some churches have paid rich dividends.

Special classes may also be planned to teach adults and young people how to work with the elementary choirs. Few churches can pay more than two or three music staff members. There is a place of service for the volunteer worker in the Music Ministry of his church.

3. *Leadership Training*

It is rare indeed to find a church which has all the trained leaders it needs for the graded choir program. Throughout the educational organizations accompanists and song leaders are needed. Few of them have the skill and training they need for doing excellent work. It is therefore the task of the church to provide training for all the leaders. Much of the field has already been covered under the two previous points, but we are now considering only the leadership.

(1) *Music schools.*—Church music schools should be held each year. All choir directors, accompanists, associates, and choir sponsors should study the *Graded Choir Handbook* and the *Church Music Manual*.

(2) *Classes or clinics.*—Leadership classes or clinics should be conducted as often as needed. Separate classes or clinics may be arranged for the workers with different age groups. These should include directors, associates, accompanists, and sponsors. Another plan is to include those who are responsible for the music in the various departments in Sunday school and Training Union.

(3) *Associational music schools.*—In some associations it is possible to have associational music schools. In others the program is not far enough advanced to have sufficient participation. The larger churches have an opportunity, through the associational schools, to encourage the smaller churches to meet their local music needs. Where the work is small it may be possible to combine the music school with other

associational training schools. There will always be an over-lapping in leadership. But this is true whether the schools are held separately or not.

(4) *Leadership conferences.*—State and Convention-wide leadership conferences offer a great opportunity for church music leaders. The state meetings will vary in length. District and associational camps use four or five days. At Ridgecrest, North Carolina, and at Glorieta, New Mexico, one week each year is provided for music leadership training. Many churches are sending their top leaders to one of these events every summer. A more technical type of conference, designed especially for music directors, is held in some of the colleges and seminaries. These various types of conferences offer excellent faculties and bring in wonderful musicians to teach and direct great choral works.

(5) *In-service training.*—Within the local church there should be a constant program of in-service training. There are many men, women, and young people who are talented in music but have had little opportunity to improve their skills. Enlist all the people you possibly can. You will be helping them and the church.

IV. CONCLUSION

1. *The Past*

Our study has revealed the antiquity of music in worship. The development of music has been uneven and spotty. Much of the time church music suffered while secular music thrived. On the other hand, there were eras when religious music crowded all other kinds into the background.

The past gave us *The Creation* (Haydn), *Elijah* (Mendelssohn), *Judas Maccabaeus, The Messiah,* and *Samson,* (Handel), Verdi's *Requiem,* Rossini's *Stabat Mater, The Passion According to St. John* and *The Passion According to St. Matthew* (Bach), and many others.

Such works have lived because they are truly great. In the present we lean heavily on the past only when the past has something that is worthy of use.

2. *The Present*

Never in the history of the world has music held such an important place. Music of every type floods the air waves. We watch and listen when artists appear on television. In almost every home some kind of record player can be found. Music stores flourish. Millions of people who cannot tolerate jazz and bop can enjoy the symphony and the opera.

The churches have been rather slow, but are now on the way toward a great music goal. Boys and girls learn music in school, at the church, and in studios, as well as in the home through music appreciation records, etc.

In more and more churches children are being trained through the graded choirs.

This upsurge of interest in music is good. The Lord is honoring the effort. Compare the music departments in Baptist colleges and seminaries with those of twenty-five years ago. Look also at the music section of the *Baptist Book Store Catalog* and compare it with the section of even ten years ago. Music is on the upward trend in our churches. More music and better music is the cry.

3. *The Bright Future*

It is evident that this growth is not a flash-in-the-pan development. It is solid, permanent. How does it happen? It is the old law of supply and demand. Churches are demanding better music. Worship is being stressed. As a result, music in worship has become of much greater importance to the people. The future is bright.

There will be better instruments and instrumentalists. There will be better-trained ministers of music and more of them. The thousands in graded choirs today will fill the choir lofts of tomorrow, and the quality of music will take a leap upward. Pastors will, of necessity, be better trained in music and in the art of worship. Denominationally, we have the leaders. In the churches there is the demand. The future is as bright as the promises of God.

PRAYER

We thank thee, Heavenly Father, for singing hearts and for voices with which to sing. We thank thee for words that have been given to us by consecrated writers and for the melodies that have been provided by Christian composers. Thou hast been so abundantly good to us; thou hast given us every reason to be happy Christian people. So, Father, let us lift up our voices and sing! Let us cultivate singing hearts that our lives may bring joy, strength, and comfort to needy hearts and lives, and above all, that we may honor thee and bring glory to thy name. Amen

FOR FURTHER STUDY AND DISCUSSION

1. Make a list of desirable pieces of equipment mentioned in this chapter. Check this list against that which is actually in your church buildings. Present the list to the pastor.
2. Check the materials, books, and other literature used in the Music Ministry of your church. What hymnals are used in the various departments? List them. What is their condition? If they are in need of repair or replacement, do something about the matter.
3. Now that you have studied this text, look at the other volumes in the series. How many have you studied? Take one and read it as a supplement to this course.
4. As a musician, or as a participant in public worship, evaluate this study in the light of your previous experiences. We hope it has been helpful.

Questions for Review and Written Work

CHAPTER 1

1. Write out your own definition of worship.
2. Outline the experience of Isaiah as related in Isaiah 6:1–8.
3. Discuss briefly what is meant by aids to worship.

CHAPTER 2

4. Name the types of musical instruments and list as many of the instruments as possible under each type.
5. Enumerate some specific contrasts of the music of the Old Testament with that of the New Testament.
6. With which Emperor did pagan music die? Describe the music of the new era.

CHAPTER 3

7. What was the major influence of Martin Luther on church music.
8. Who were the Huguenots, and what were their contributions to early church music?
9. Define chorale, anthem, opera, oratorio, and cantata.
10. Write a short statement on the subject, "The Music I Like Best."

CHAPTER 4

11. Briefly describe your church, its size, its buildings and equipment, and its program.
12. How would you attempt to make God real to a congregation?
13. Describe the auditorium of your church as you see it when you are participating in a worship service.

CHAPTER 5

14. Define: prelude, invocation, anthem, offertory, and postlude.
15. Make out an order of service for morning worship as you would like it.
16. Make out an order of service for the evening service according to your own desire.

CHAPTER 6

17. Why is the place of the minister of music a difficult one?
18. List the various tasks which may challenge a minister of music.

19. What is the work of the accompanist?
20. From your own experience give a good example of teamwork.

CHAPTER 7

21. Make out a brief agenda which could be wisely followed in a worship service planning conference.
22. Where should choir rehearsals be held? What should be the procedure? When is the rehearsal held in your church? Why?
23. What spiritual preparation should be made by the various leaders of church worship?

CHAPTER 8

24. List the "special days" recognized in your church.
25. List five of your favorite hymns for Christmas services.
26. How do revival services differ from the usual Sunday services?

CHAPTER 9

27. What part does equipment play in making worship services effective?

28. List as many available pieces of music literature as you can, including books, magazines, and hymnals.
29. What music texts are available for church music schools? List the ones you have studied.
30. If you were giving guidance to one who felt called to give his full time to the church Music Ministry how would you answer these questions: What opportunities are available in the area of church music as a Christian vocation? How does one prepare himself for this work? What are some of the responsibilities of the minister of music in a church?